Billy Rose Presents...
CASA MANANA

Billy Rose Presents... CASA MANANA

BY
JAN JONES

TCU PRESS

FORT WORTH, TEXAS

Library of Congress Cataloging-in Publication Data

Jones, Jan, 1947-
    Billy Rose Present— Casa Manana / by Jan Jones.
      p. c.m. — (Chisholm Trail series ; no. 20)
    Includes bibliographical references and index.
    ISBN 0-87565-199-2 (cloth) 0-87565-201-8 (alk. Paper)
    1. Fort Worth (Tex.)—History—20th century. 2. Texas—Centennial celebrations, etc.
3. Rose, Billy, 1899-1966. 4. Casa Manana (Fort Worth, Tex.)—History. 5. Fort Worth
(Tex.)—Buildings, structure, etc. I. Title. II. Series.
    F394.F7 J66 .1999
    976.4'5315—ddc21

                                                98-42827
                                                   CIP

Cover and text design by Bill Maize; Duo Design Group

Jacket illustration from cover of 1937 Frontier Fiesta program

Correspondence from the Macmillan files about *Gone With The Wind* is used by permission of the
New York Public Library and G.W.T.W. Literary Rights.

The photo of Sally Rand on page 115 is used by permission from the Billy Rose Theatre Collection, The
New York Public Library for the Performing Arts, Astor, Lenox and Tilden Foundations.

The quote from *Jumbo* on page 22 is copyright © 1934 by Ben Hecht and Charles MacArthur,
renewed in 1961 by Helen Hayes MacArthur and is reprinted by permission of the William Morris
Agency, Inc., on behalf of the Author.

* * * * * *

FOR MY PARENTS AND FOR RICK

WHO CONTINUED TO BELIEVE IN THE PROJECT

AND

TO ALL THE DANCERS, SHOWGIRLS, AND SHOWBOYS

OF THE CASA MAÑANA REVUE 1936-1939

WHO INSPIRED ME WITH THEIR STORIES

* * * * * *

CONTENTS ....

ACKNOWLEDGMENTS · · · · · · · · · · · ·

In 1985 Dr. Rick Selcer proposed a project to a group of local writers and historians—writing a series of books preserving various aspects of Fort Worth history. My connection to the group seemed tenuous at best—I was a high-school English and theater instructor. He knew that several years before I had completed a master's thesis on Casa Mañana Musicals, Inc., an organization inspired by Billy Rose's Casa Mañana. While fewer than twenty pages of my original thesis had been devoted to that earlier event, Rick proposed expanding the section on Rose's tenure in Fort Worth into a book, despite my skepticism that enough material could be located. At one discouraging point, I laid the manuscript aside for several years, but at every opportunity Rick continued to insist that I resurrect it before all the living witnesses were gone. In the end, it was his persistence and belief in the project that kept it alive.

As this project evolved through several years and numerous changes in direction, I was aided in my research by many organizations and individuals who provided me with both technical advice and criticism. Dee Barker of the Tarrant County Historical Commission and Ruby Schmidt, past president of the Tarrant County Historical Society, were both helpful in directing me to new sources and allowing me access to many one-of-a-kind artifacts. I also owe a large debt of thanks to Jane Klazura and Jane Boley of the Special Collections Library, University of Texas at Arlington. Both helped me navigate the *Fort Worth Star-Telegram* photo archives and patiently searched for alternatives when I could not find exactly what I wanted. The Amon Carter Foundation and Ruth Carter Stevenson graciously allowed me access to the Amon Carter papers, a collection which is without doubt the largest surviving record of the day-to-day operations of Casa Mañana and the Frontier Centennial. In addition, Mrs. Stevenson read the manuscript, corrected errors, and provided insights from the viewpoint of a witness with close connections to many of the personalities involved in the events of 1936 and 1937. Paula Stewart, director of the archives at the Amon

Carter Museum, helped me narrow my search through her knowledge of the Carter collection. Sending me in new directions, she undoubtedly saved me countless hours. The staff of the Fort Worth Public Library's local history department answered my questions, searched through their collections for related materials, and repeatedly dragged out the Casa Mañana scrapbooks, each of which must weigh at least thirty pounds. I also received invaluable assistance from the staffs of Dallas Public Library, Southwestern Baptist Theological Seminary Library, Ohio Historical Society, Cleveland State University Library, University of Georgia Library, University of Texas Center for American History, New York Public Library, and New York Public Library for the Performing Arts at Lincoln Center.

Without taking credit from those mentioned earlier, I value most the individuals who gave time to share their memories—Jack Gordon, Mary Wynn Wayman, Melvin Dacus, Michael Polluck, Phil North, William Jary, Ronald Aultman, Ruth Carter Stevenson—and all the former showgirls, dancers and employees of the Frontier Centennial and the Casa Mañana Revue—Janice Nicolson Holmes, Olive Nicolson Pemberton, Norris Mefford and Dorothy Murray Mefford, Beth Lea Clardy, Wilby Lingo Goodman, Mary Paige Covey Oliver, and Virginia Dofflemeyer Miller. They have given me a new perspective on Fort Worth's rich historical legacy.

INTRODUCTION · · · · · · · · · · · ·

It was a swelteringly hot midsummer day in 1936. West of the Trinity River bluffs, construction was well under way on the grounds of the Fort Worth Frontier Centennial. Several hundred concessionaires, electricians, painters, and carpenters toiled, oblivious to the visible waves of heat rising from the parched blackland prairie. Grateful to be working anywhere in the depths of the Great Depression, they labored feverishly against an opening set for July 18, now less than ten days away. Overseeing the controlled mayhem of preparations was an odd little chain-smoking figure in elevator shoes. Thirty-five-year-old Billy Rose, a New York nightclub entrepreneur and sometime Broadway producer, had been hired by a committee of local businessmen to coordinate Fort Worth's contribution to the Texas Centennial celebration. This particular afternoon Rose conducted a frenetic walking tour of the grounds accompanied by his wife, actress Fanny Brice, herself one of the most beloved entertainers of the New York theater scene. Here, 1,200 miles from the heart of Broadway, in a western city still strongly connected to its frontier legacy of cattle drives, desperadoes, and cowpunchers, Rose intended to stage his most recent theatrical enterprise, innocuously titled "Frontier Follies." To insure the success of this venture, investors had guaranteed Rose a personal salary of $100,000 and built him an astonishing theater. Taking the advice of his frequent collaborator, stage director John Murray Anderson, Rose named the new structure Casa Mañana, the "House of Tomorrow," and in keeping with its title, his design team complemented the building with a lagoon and water curtain, a full-service restaurant, a fifty-foot bar, innovative lighting and sound equipment, and a state-of-the-art revolving-reciprocating stage nearly the size of a city block.[1] When Rose led Fanny inside the 4,000-seat open-air amphitheater, the centennial's centerpiece attraction, she reportedly exclaimed, "Oh, Billy, it's a goose's dream!"

Brice's allusion to the golden egg of fairy tale would not have been lost on Fort Worth centennial planners. The exhibition Brice had traveled from New

York to see had undergone a dramatic transformation in concept during the winter of 1936 with the hiring of Rose. The improbable turn in events began with the Fort Worth planners' seeking a more effective way to infuse into the local economy some of the millions in tourist dollars being generated by the official celebration of the Texas Centennial, already underway in Dallas. At the urging of Metro-Goldwyn-Mayer executive Rufus Le Maire, several prominent and influential local businessmen, including Amon G. Carter, Sr., William Monnig, Marvin D. Evans, and James M. North, Jr., arranged a meeting with Billy Rose. Rose, on hiatus in California after a money-losing but critically acclaimed Broadway production of the musical *Jumbo*, was eventually persuaded to take on the project. As part of the deal, Rose reassembled much of his *Jumbo* production team, sets, cast, and crew and moved the entire operation to Fort Worth. Originally intended as a modest "pioneer days" celebration, the Frontier Centennial, exploded into an improbable conglomeration of agricultural exhibits, sideshow nudes, an old-time Wild West show, the musicalized circus *Jumbo*, and a parade of Broadway and vaudeville talent led by feature artiste, stripper Sally Rand. It was a spectacle to make Florenz Ziegfeld envious. The scale and sheer audacity of Casa Mañana made Billy Rose, already becoming known as "The Barnum of the Age," a national celebrity and helped solidify his growing reputation as a showman.

"*Fort Worth For Entertainment; Dallas For Education.*" That open challenge, pasted and splashed across the Southwest on billboards, gas station walls, and weathered barns, fired the imagination of the public but angered Dallas centennial officials seeking to maintain the higher level of decorum befitting a memorial to heroes who fought and died in the Texas Revolution. Despite the controversy, or perhaps in part because of it, the publicity brought over a million Depression-weary funseekers to Fort Worth over the next four years. They came mainly to see Casa Mañana, a theater that in 1936 was unique both in concept and in scale.

In the process of bringing notoriety to both Fort Worth and Dallas and embellishing his own reputation as a showman, Rose accomplished something else. Armed with unrestricted control as director-general, a sometimes brusque manner, and often controversial notions of how best to attract audiences, he managed to change the character of the state celebration and forced centennial planners to reevaluate their marketing strategies—Dallas announced plans for its own rodeo and adults-only sideshows. *Variety*, the entertainment industry trade publication, took note of the changes, reflecting, "Without the advent of Mr. Rose in Fort Worth and his theories filtering over to Dallas, the Dallas Centennial might have been rather stuffy, too busy expounding the adventures of the mind to give proper attention to enticements of the body."[2]

If Billy Rose's idea for Casa Mañana quickly became an anachronism, the fault lay partly with Rose himself. By the very next year, Rose began outdoing Rose with variations on the Casa Mañana format—his fabulous Aquacades in Cleveland (1937) and San Francisco (1940) and the 1939 New York World's Fair. In New York he even opened the Casa Mañana nightclub, importing many of the original Texas performers for its stage show. Except in personal accounts of Rose, his press agent Richard Maney, and Casa Mañana's director, John Murray Anderson, many theater historians erroneously place the improbable events of 1936 in Dallas rather than Fort Worth or confuse them with Rose's later successes. The Frontier Centennial and its sequel, the Frontier Fiesta, closed after only two brief seasons (1936 and 1937), the second season cut short by controversy and lawsuits. Rose himself departed under a cloud, informed by city fathers that his services were no longer required. Casa Mañana stumbled on under independent management companies for two more seasons but finally closed at the end of 1939 as the growing certainty of global war loomed.

After Casa Mañana, Rose continued to expand his reputation as an innovator, became a multimillionaire through shrewd investment, and by the time of his death in 1966 had achieved almost legendary status in the world of theatrical production. Yet in both form and formula he continued to recreate Casa Mañana, his mammoth cabaret centerpiece for the Texas Frontier Centennial, for the rest of his life.

Rose returned to Fort Worth only once—in 1954. The thirteen members of the Fort Worth Frontier Centennial board of control honored him with a testimonial luncheon where he confided to a *Star-Telegram* reporter, "Fort Worth sort of solidified everything. The Casa Mañana gave me the formula. Almost every-thing good that's happened to me since stemmed from what happened here."[3] Later, the group took Rose on a tour of the old exposition grounds, now com-pletely razed except for one building, the Pioneer Palace. A decaying, star-shaped water fountain, still standing where Casa Mañana's main entrance had been, was all that remained to mark where the theater had once stood. Rose turned to his old friend, newspaperman Jack Gordon, and remarked bitterly, "If you ever write anything about this junkyard, don't forget to mention that I had the world's longest bar in my Casa Mañana—now that's something a man would like to be remembered for."[4]

THE WAR FOR CENTENNIAL DOLLARS

Pre-opening publicity for the Frontier Centennial pronounced it modestly, *"The Biggest Enterprise Devoted Exclusively To Amusement In The History Of The World. . . ."* Glaring full-page ads invited patrons to "Dine and Dance under the Milky Way to the strains of Paul Whiteman's Band and Bask in the Effulgence of Brightest Luminaries of Stage, Screen and Radio Flanked by a Bewilderingly Beautiful Ensemble of 200 Delectable Girls."[1]

Writer Damon Runyon declared its dazzling centerpiece, Casa Mañana, "probably the biggest and most original show ever seen in these United States."[2] On opening night, July 18, 1936, spectators, awed by the sheer immensity of the spectacle, reportedly left drinks and dinners untouched as several dozen statuesque showgirls and dancers paraded through production numbers on a stage more than three times larger than that of Radio City Music Hall. Even the forces of nature seemed under the sway of the show's magic. As Everett Marshall crooned, "The night is young and you're so beautiful," to Texas' Number One Sweetheart, Faye Cotton, the moon rose as if on cue behind the outdoor cabaret theater. This fortuitous conjunction of the natural with the theatrical moved one patron to comment, "It's a mad-man's dream," a statement tinged with more than a little irony, because the mercurial force behind this Texas-size extravaganza was a diminutive New Yorker dubbed by his own press agent the "Bantam Barnum," William Samuel Rosenberg—a.k.a., Billy Rose.

The Fort Worth Frontier Centennial and Casa Mañana began innocently enough as merely one of many festivals planned statewide in 1936 to celebrate the centennial anniversary of Texas' independence from Mexico. Preparations for the event had begun more than a decade before with the establishment of the Centennial Governing Board of One Hundred, a committee created in 1924 to provide organizational and administrative structure for the movement as various centennial concepts were first proposed and then discarded or revised. The committee members, sixty-two of whom were elected from the state's thirty-one senatorial districts, with the remainder appointed to serve at-large, had as their major duties publicizing and naming the event, educating the general public to the centennial's importance, and conducting a statewide industrial survey. All of this was necessary to prepare for the formal presentation of a funding proposal to the state legislature. The very next year, the movement, in fact, received official recognition from the thirty-ninth legislature with the passage of House Concurrent Resolution No. 11, but monetary appropriations were still not forthcoming. The selection of Houston financier and philanthropist Jesse H. Jones as director-general of the board seemed to assure an early resolution to the problem of funding, but Jones' reluctance to move forward with definitive blueprints for the centennial extended throughout the nearly four years of his tenure and ran directly counter to the statewide enthusiasm other members of the board had worked so hard to build.[3]

In the meantime, the stock-market crash of October 1929 effectively erased much of the impetus the centennial movement had gained through the formation of the board and the appointment of Jones as director. As the effects of the crash deepened, unemployment spread rapidly throughout the country and retail spending declined. Between 1929 and 1932, an estimated 85,000 American companies went bankrupt, leaving as many as twelve million people out of work.[4] The spending of millions of dollars on a statewide historical pageant began to seem frivolous by comparison. Further complicating matters, the Texas constitution specifically prohibited the use of state funds to support fairs and expositions of any type.

The establishment of the permanent Texas Centennial Committee and the appointment of its twenty-one-member executive board was consequently delayed until 1931. At the same time the centennial movement was gaining this renewed vigor, Jesse H. Jones chose to announce his resignation as director-general to accept appointment to the board of Reconstruction Finance Corporation. He was replaced by Dallas attorney Cullen F. Thomas. Not until November of 1932 did the issue of centennial funding finally reach Texas voters in the form of a referendum election. By a margin of 59,000 votes Texans approved an amendment to the state constitution allowing the legislature to appropriate state funds for the centennial. Despite the approbation of voters, over a year after the passage of the referendum, Thomas complained to Fort Worth committee member Amon G. Carter that the board was still "resting on arms for lack of financial support."[5]

It was February of 1934 before the Texas House voted officially to accept and fund Senate Bill No. 22. Even then, legislators intially earmarked only $100,000 from state coffers. The legislature, both in acknowledgment of its economic obligations to constituents and intending perhaps to head off squabbling among various special-interest groups, next declared that no one city could rightfully establish sole claim as most prominent in the war for independence. The criteria for settling the question of where the central exhibition would be located were reduced for all practical purposes to one critical issue—money. This ambivalence on the part of legislators—promoting commemoration of the centennial on the one hand yet seeking to shift its funding elsewhere—no doubt contributed to another seven-month delay in finalizing the choice of site for the celebration. Not until after the centennial appropriation bill officially became law in June of 1934 did the State Centennial Committee finally convene at Austin's Driskill Hotel to begin hearings on what form the exhibition should take and to settle the issue of what city would host the pageant.[6]

While the slow, deliberate actions of the legislature demonstrated political and fiscal caution in a decade of unprecedented hardship, the decision to award the plum central exhibition to the community offering the "greatest financial inducement" removed from consideration all but a handful of potential sites. Several cities, notably Houston with its San Jacinto battlefield, objected strongly to this pecuniary stance, adopted as many saw it, at the expense of patriotism. Committee officers, led by director-general Thomas, nevertheless remained adamant that a strict interpretation of state law precluded any historical considerations.[7] The

Fort Worth Star-Telegram, owned by committee member Amon G. Carter and long a public supporter of funding the centennial because of potential economic benefits to the state, had come out publicly in support of either San Antonio or Houston. However managing editor James M. North noted that this move contradicted other local interests lobbying either for Fort Worth or a site midway between the city and its neighbor and rival thirty miles to the east, Dallas.[8]

Following several open hearings across the state in the summer of 1934 during which invited historians and representative citizens addressed the centennial committee, members were in agreement on one central issue: the exhibition should "impressively emphasize the material, educational, artistic, cultural, and religious development of the people of Texas." Local pageants should be "interwoven intimately with the early romantic history of Texas . . . in the holding of the Central Exposition and historical celebrations, all of them [should] be conducted in the spirit of cooperation."[9] At the conclusion of the hearings, the committee invited several cities, including Fort Worth, to submit bids to host the central exhibition, but by the September 1 deadline only three—Houston, Dallas, and San Antonio—offered proposals. Each in turn was asked the same question: would the city have the ability and willingness to carry out plans for the exhibition even if state or federal aid was not forthcoming? Houston, complaining that such a plan would produce a local fair, not a Texas centennial, estimated that it would require at least $3 million in matching funds from the state to carry out its proposal. San Antonio requested underwriting of at least $1 million, ironically leaving only Dallas, a town that did not even exist in 1836, to come away victorious in the centennial war.[10]

The "war" turned out to be little more than a skirmish. As the financial capital of Texas, Dallas simply had bigger guns and outflanked all rivals, offering nearly $8 million for the honor.[11] Dallas banker Robert L. Thornton brazenly proclaimed to the committee, "We've got the plant, we've got the money, and to show our pride in Texas, we've got the guts to spend it."[12] Eventually the losing communities managed to recoup some of their damaged civic pride through state and federal grants. Houston received $400,000 to memorialize the Battle of San Jacinto, and San Antonio, $440,000 for repair of the Alamo. Fort Worth, largely through the influence of *Star-Telegram* publisher Amon G. Carter, dry-goods entrepreneur William Monnig, and other prominent citizens, wangled a modest $250,000 from the Commission of Control for the Texas Centennial Celebrations to produce what promised to be a well-intentioned if unremarkable sideshow mélange of exhibits including a casino, a pioneer village, a museum for display of "historic relics and curios," and a band shell for symphony concerts, all blandly packaged as the "Livestock and Frontier Days Exposition." In October of 1935 the Fort Worth City Council adopted a resolution declaring " . . . an emergency existing for the construction of the Centennial Stock Show buildings due to the fact that the Centennial opens in Texas in the summer of 1936 making it necessary to the best interests of the City of Fort Worth that construction be immediately started on said projects." The council petitioned the Public Works Administration to reapportion $1,550,000 in pending grants affecting various Fort Worth municipal projects, temporarily sidelining plans for a new city hall and library but making available $725,000 in additional funds for centennial buildings, with the remaining $825,000 going for airport improvements and a tuberculosis sanitorium.[13] The funds eventually raised totaled $1,862,727, with $887,000 coming from city bond elections, $250,000 from federal centennial funds, and from the PWA grant, $725,727. Amon Carter, in a letter to Fort Worth Congressman Fritz Lanham proclaimed, "It is our purpose to build the finest exposition grounds to be found anywhere in the United States . . . giving the evolution of the cattle business from the early mission days up to the present time, using the old Longhorn steers, Indians, and other such things typical of the old trail driving frontier days."[14]

As the awarding of state and federal funds commenced, any pretense of the "spirit of cooperation" between communities vanished. Dallas' reaction was immediate and bitter after the announcement of the grant to Fort Worth. Correspondent William F. Thornton of the *Dallas Morning News* complained that the $250,000 allotted to the city "for its proposed memorial to the livestock industry of Texas" had placed it "above Gonzales and Goliad," sites granted only $50,000 apiece for memorialization of the Fannin massacre and the first shot for independence. The grant had the effect, he grumbled, of placing Fort Worth "on parity with San Antonio and its Alamo and Houston, where was fought the Battle of San Jacinto, one of the seven decisive battles of the world."[15]

Thornton's reaction simply reflected that of several members of the centennial's historical advisory board. Immediately after the announcement of the Fort Worth grant, three members of the board, including its chairman Lou W. Kemp and historian J. Frank Dobie, resigned in protest. They did not take exception so much to the commemoration of the livestock industry as to what they perceived as a disproportional allotment to one city when state grant funds were severely limited.[16]

While the partisan wrangling over historical grants continued, choice of an appropriate site for the Fort Worth exhibition was becoming equally contentious for local centennial planners. The Fort Worth Stock Yards Company lobbied strongly to keep the centennial in North Fort Worth on the existing site of the Fat Stock Show and Rodeo.

Among various alternative locations submitted to the council for consideration was the 138-acre Van Zandt tract along the Clear Fork of the Trinity River.[17] K. M. Van Zandt, Fort Worth pioneer and civic leader who moved to the city shortly after the end of the Civil War, homesteaded the site in 1872. Van Zandt and others led the struggling frontier community during its transformation into an important crossroads of the southwestern cattle industry. The Van Zandt section lay on the eastern edge of what had been Camp Bowie, an army training base established in 1917 during World War I and then abandoned at war's end in 1918. To the south lay Rock Springs Park, to the east, Trinity Park and the Clear Fork river bluffs, and to the west and north were the neighborhoods of Arlington Heights, Monticello, Rose Hill, and Crestmount, which had sprung up as the site of the old base was parceled out to developers.[18]

Representatives of the North Side went so far as to accuse city council members of holding closed-door meetings with Amon Carter, who already held an option on the Van Zandt homestead. Council members admitted meeting with Carter but denied having discussed the Van Zandt site and, after examining several alternate locations, initially voted to accept the stockyards location. The matter appeared settled, but in November 1935 architects began to raise serious questions concerning the size of the proposed tract (thirty-two acres) and the improvements necessary to stabilize the site. They advised that additional land would be needed. The city council accepted the recommendations, a fateful decision leading to a dividing of the centennial between two locations. A planned centennial stock show would remain in North Fort Worth, but other exhibits and entertainment facilities would be moved to a second site.[19]

City council members at first could not reach agreement with the heirs on a purchase price for the old homestead but finally struck a compromise when family members agreed to deduct the payment of back taxes from the selling price.[20] On December 18 the city council adopted a resolution authorizing purchase of the property for $150,000. As part of the contract, the city council agreed to a pair of curious deed restrictions governing the sale: the land could never be resold to "negroes" or ever used as a cemetery. An additional restriction against the sale of alcoholic beverages did not apply to the actual Frontier Days site. Plans called for a complete restoration of the old Van Zandt farmhouse.[21]

In late December 1935 the city council appointed a board of control to handle the day-to-day operations of the centennial. Spearheading the creation of the exposition were some of Fort Worth's most prominent citizens, including board of control president, William Monnig; vice president, Marvin D. Evans; secretary and general manager, John B. Davis; and treasurer, W. L. Pier. Others serving included T. J. Harrell, Mayor Van Zandt Jarvis, who was also manager of the stock show, Jerome C. Martin, James M. North, Jr., O. B. Sellers, Seward P. Sheldon, John N. Sparks, and Edward H. Winton.

For all its sincerity the Fort Worth Frontier Days Exposition seemed destined for a rather ignominious demise. Despite two bond elections in September 1935 and January 1936, Fort Worth still had committed less than a million dollars in local funds to finance its centennial enterprise. Additional government funding also proved slow in coming through: city fathers could not reach agreement with architects on final plans for submission to the PWA.[22] By March 1936, with the scheduled opening of the $25-million Dallas exposition only three months away, some members of the local board spoke out publicly in favor of abandoning the entire project.

Amon G. Carter, Sr., a citizen of singular personality and unquestioned influence, did not share those feelings. Carter viewed the naming of Dallas as the site of the centennial exposition a gross miscarriage of justice and determined to get even by mounting a show that would directly rival the "official" celebration. Both Carter and Mrs. Bob Barker had been named to serve as representatives from Fort Worth on the Texas Centennial Committee, but Carter attended none of the committee's planning sessions nor did he take part in any actions leading to the selection of Dallas as the site.[23] Whether by design or because of previous commitments, he was frequently absent from the state during most of the deliberations. However, Carter's well-documented disdain of Dallas can probably be blamed at least in part for his decision to take no part in committee proceedings, despite cajoling by committee President Cullen Thomas, who pleaded for his "dynamic, Texanic, aid in this great enterprise in behalf of all Texas." [24]

Despite his limited participation, even in the early planning stages Carter could seldom resist promoting Fort Worth's frontier exhibition at the expense of rival Dallas. In 1935 he suggested to the commission that a statue of William F. Cody sculpted by Gertrude Vanderbilt Whitney and proposed for the Dallas centennial grounds might seem inappropriate since Cody was not even a Texan. In attempting to requisition the statue, Carter began by observing, "While I have not been given credit for lying awake nights trying to help Dallas, at the same time the Centennial is an all-state endeavor and one so beneficial that like every other Texan I am interested in its success." He went on to suggest that the legendary scout would be far more at home in the frontier setting of Fort Worth and generously offered to take charge of the sculpture, saying, "I fear a hardy old plainsman such as he might not feel at home in the city atmosphere of Dallas."[25] Carter might have been right in attempting to appropriate the statue. A lawsuit filed by Austin oilman C. L. Greenwood alleging that Cody was a traitor and Union spy delayed the placement of the statue on the centennial grounds for several months. Greenwood's attorney claimed that " . . . a statue of Hitler [or] Mussolini would be as appropriate as one of Buffalo Bill." It took the State Court of Civil Appeals to settle the controversy.[26]

While William Monnig and the frontier board possessed the business acumen necessary for dealing with design, construction, and funding, Carter, gregarious, sometimes impulsive, and outspoken, had far more "hands on" experience at one-upmanship. He had earned a reputation for staging colorful publicity stunts intended to promote the growth of his city and thereby increase the circulation of his newspaper. Until his death in 1955, Carter served as self-appointed ambassador-at-large from Fort Worth to the rest of the world, gaining notoriety for the city through flamboyant boosterism and well-publicized friendships with Franklin D. Roosevelt and actor-humorist Will Rogers.

When other prominent backers favored cancelling the project as bills and problems mounted, Carter's zeal and influence undoubtedly provided the impetus necessary to push the Fort Worth Centennial and Casa Mañana to completion, ultimately bringing the city and its exhibition to national prominence in the summer of 1936.

"IN TEXAS THE CHILDREN ARE VERY PRECOCIOUS"

John Nance Garner, two-term vice president of the United States under Franklin Roosevelt, once commented about his friend Amon Carter: "[He] wants the government of the United States run for the exclusive benefit of Fort Worth and, if possible, to the detriment of Dallas."[1] The *Dallas Morning News* bore further testimony to the accuracy of Garner's remark in 1939, jokingly bestowing honorary citizenship status on Carter "because he punched Dallas like cowboys are wont to do slow steers in a shipping chute."[2] The paper returned to a similar theme sixteen years later to write Carter's obituary. In an era when his record of civic and governmental influence had yet to be eclipsed by the ascendancy of Lyndon Johnson and other Texans of more notoriety, the *News* staff acknowledged Carter as ". . . perhaps the most internationally famous Texan of the 20th century," noting almost incidentally that ". . . through his aggressiveness for his beloved Fort Worth, Carter was a great stimulant to Dallas businessmen."[3]

Taken as a body, the comments testify to Amon Carter's seemingly epic tenacity in matters affecting the development of Fort Worth yet still manage to understate the extent of his obsession with a civic rivalry which in fact had begun many years before Carter arrived on the scene in 1905. The feud between the burgeoning frontier communities of Fort Worth and Dallas, situated only thirty miles apart on the three forks of the Trinity River, had its origins in skirmishes over issues often contested by neighboring cities: competition for settlers, trade, and the necessary community services and amenities that attracted these. Dallas, a considerably older settlement, had its beginnings as a trading post established on the east bank of the Trinity by John Neely Bryan in 1840. First surveyed in 1846, it was chartered by the state as a town in 1856 and achieved city status in 1871. Fort Worth, not even officially incorporated until March 1, 1873, came into existence in 1849 as the last in a series of six military outposts established north and west of San Antonio by the war department. Situated along 300 miles of the Balcones Escarpment, the forts secured what were then the remotest perimeters of the Texas frontier. Fort Worth survived abandonment by the army and the Civil War years as an isolated village of 300, owing its survival at least in part to the impetus it gained in snatching the county seat designation away from nearby Birdville, first in 1856 and again in 1860.[4] By the year of Fort Worth's incorporation, Dallas already had a population of 3,000, further bolstered by the acquisition of two railways—the Houston and Texas Central and the Texas & Pacific. In one year, from 1872 to 1873, Fort Worth increased in population from only a few hundred to three or four thousand in anticipation of the arrival of the Texas & Pacific Railroad. But after the roadbed reached Eagle Ford, just west of Dallas, a national financial panic struck, halting the railroad's planned expansion to Fort Worth. Adding insult to injury, many of Fort Worth's newly acquired citizens, fearing bankruptcy, abandoned businesses and homes and moved to Dallas.[5]

The rivalry as a significant source of irritation as well as civic pride can be traced to one of Amon Carter's predecessors, Fort Worth newspaper editor and mayor Buckley B. Paddock, an erudite self-educated lawyer, politician, and writer who became embroiled in local municipal causes soon after emigrating to Fort Worth from Mississippi in the early 1870s. He purchased the *Fort Worth Democrat* and through its pages spearheaded the campaign that eventually succeeded in extending the much delayed Texas & Pacific railhead to the town in July 1876. This civic coup sparked an economic boom that helped transform the sleepy village into a bustling center for the cattle industry and led to the construction of churches, an opera house, a new courthouse (to replace one that had burned earlier), a permanent city hall, and, ironically, a flourishing red-light district,

Hell's Half Acre. The Dallas press ignored the progress, instead casting its westerly neighbor as homely and dull, a virtual shantytown. Paddock, in his turn, regularly excoriated Dallas' self-important vitriol, taking sarcastic jabs at its exposed underbelly: "Matters seem to be growing desperate about Dallas. Murders and robberies are so frequent that the daily papers of that city are little more than local reporters of desperate and daring crimes."[6] The *Austin Statesman* took note of the rancorous undercurrents in late 1876 when it reported an incident involving Paddock that not only attested to the city's ongoing problems with isolation but revealed the extent of the antipathy already existing between the two communities: "Dallas people made the agent of Callender's Minstrels believe that Fort Worth was no bigger than one's fist, and the minstrels concluded not to go thither. . . . Paddock heard of the outrage, had the census taken and houses counted and the minstrels were roped in. Paddock is perfectly blest, and Dallas is in sackcloth and ashes."[7]

Over the next thirty years, Fort Worth transformed itself from a frontier jumping-off point to a booming center of the cattle and livestock industry. No fewer than nine separate railways formed a hub extending out from the city in a network that reached not only into several surrounding states but connected the region's ranching and agricultural enterprises to the major midwestern markets in Chicago and St. Louis.[8] In 1903 Swift and Armour opened meat-packing operations adjacent to the city's stockyards. In addition the city had two daily newspapers and a population that had exploded from 6,600 in 1880 to over 26,000 in 1900.

Amon Carter's alliance with the city began in 1905. He opened an agency selling streetcar advertising but shortly branched out into a job with one of the town's three daily newspapers, the *Star*. Since he was the struggling rag's only advertising salesman, he also gained the title of advertising manager. The *Star* had for several years fought a losing battle against its larger and better financed competitors, the *Telegram* and the *Record*. When a short time later Carter learned that local investors were interested in starting an afternoon daily, he thought of the *Star*. While he had no money to invest himself, he knew his sales ability had helped keep the *Star* afloat. Carter astutely aligned himself with several influential investors including Paul Waples and Colonel Louis J. Wortham, offering his continued services as advertising manager for an increase in salary. Colonel Wortham readily accepted the offer, and the two continued their alliance even after many of the original investors pulled out as the *Star* continued to founder. When it became clear that the little daily was in a hopeless situation against its more powerful competition, Carter and Wortham came up with a scheme to buy out one of their chief rivals—the *Telegram*. Carter helped negotiate the merger and persuaded Paul Waples and other new investors to infuse much-needed cash into the deal. As an incentive to stay with the new venture, Carter accepted a percentage of the operation with option to buy more. In 1908 the *Star-Telegram* was born, with Louis Wortham serving as publisher and editor and Amon Carter continuing as ad salesman. Several other young men including James North, A. L. Shulman, James Record, Bert Honea and Harold Hough came aboard in these early years. With Carter, they eventually became the managing staff of the paper, building it by 1913 into the fourth-largest newspaper in Texas. With the retirement of Wortham in 1923, Carter acquired control of the paper, serving as president and publisher until 1952.[9]

Amon Carter's strengths lay in his ability to build friendships with powerful individuals and then to translate those friendships into influence to be wielded almost exclusively to benefit his city. Rarely did important business executives, military brass, or government officials pass through Fort Worth without a visit to his Shady Oak Farm on Lake Worth, where each VIP duly surrendered personal headgear in exchange for a new "Shady Oak" 5X beaver Stetson, specially commissioned from Fort Worth haberdasher Washer Brothers. Carter kept a ready supply of the hats in all sizes at his home, at the *Star-Telegram*, and in his suite at the Fort Worth Club. He was fond of cautioning all new honorees, "Be careful where you leave it—my name is on it."[10] The hats Carter collected over the years from such luminaries as Franklin Roosevelt and Harry Truman, aviator Charles Lindbergh, Lord Rothermere, Prince Bernhard of the Netherlands, New York Mayor Jimmy Walker, and financier Otto Kahn reflect the level of relationships he cultivated to good advantage in advancing important civic projects. Through his personal efforts Carter persuaded Convair, Bell Aircraft, and General Motors to build plants in Fort Worth, with Carswell Air Force Base and several major oil companies following.[11]

In addition to his newspaper holdings, Carter's ability to influence also benefitted enormously from changes occurring in the commercial aviation industry. Carter moved quickly to capitalize on these changes, hoping to enhance Fort Worth's position in the jockeying between cities for major air routes. In the process, he heightened the long-simmering feud with Dallas. When Aviation Corporation, a private holding company organized by Averill Harriman and Robert Lehman, came into existence in 1929, Amon Carter was named one of its sixty-three directors. Avco, one of several such companies established following the success of Charles Lindbergh's transatlantic flight, was funded by $35 million raised through the public sale of two million shares of common stock. Formed ostensibly to coordinate and integrate development and experimental work in commercial aviation, massive entities such as Avco and Boeing quickly swallowed up regional airlines and related service companies, businesses which had no chance of competing against the new conglomerates. Avco managed to gain control of eleven of the twenty-five air-mail routes that had been opened up nationally by the government before the holding companies themselves were broken up by President Roosevelt and Congress. When this occurred, Carter pulled off what was possibly his biggest coup on behalf of the city, snatching American Airways, previously a subsidiary of Avco, away from Dallas. The company eventually changed its name to American Airlines, with Carter its largest stockholder.[12]

As Carter expanded his spheres of influence, he became adept at using the longstanding civic rivalry to the clear benefit of Fort Worth. The *Saturday Evening Post* observed, "Amon Carter's biography is a textbook for chambers of commerce and for old-fashioned town boosters. It is also a sort of military manual on how to conduct a war between two cities."[13] When Carter in 1934 persuaded American Airlines to shift its base of operations from Dallas to Fort Worth, the *Dallas Evening Journal* managed to grumble while still clearly acknowledging Carter's adroitness in pulling off the deal:

"The leadership of Dallas has been bested again in the contest for air headquarters of the Southwest. Once more we have been Amon Cartered. Dallas furnishes the passengers and the mail and the destination for passengers and mail over-whelmingly, as compared to Fort Worth. But Fort Worth furnished Amon Carter." [14]

Carter's frequent insistence on favored status for Fort Worth sometimes engendered real resentment in the Dallas business community and slowed progress on issues where cooperation between the two cities might have benefited both. The distribution of centennial funds and the choice of Dallas as the site of the central exhibition were relatively minor issues because Fort Worth and Dallas both stood to gain from their close proximity to each other. A more serious legacy of the ongoing competition was the acrimonious airport stalemate that simmered between the two cities for decades. In the early 1940s it appeared that Fort Worth and Dallas were close to reaching an agreement to build a new airport midway between the two cities, a plan that would have contributed to the regional growth of aviation and alleviated the problem of growing congestion around Dallas' Love Field. The plan fell apart, however, not to be revived for over a quarter century, after Dallas civic leaders learned that, because of pressure applied by Carter to the Civil Aeronautics Board, many of the new facility's hangars and support buildings were to be built closer to Fort Worth than Dallas.[15]

Carter's tactics alternately bewildered and amazed friends and acquaintances and led detractors to denounce what they interpreted as flagrant self-promotion. Yet beneath this streak of supposed egocentrism Carter unabashedly held to his single-minded, unshakeable purpose—bringing notice to Fort Worth, even at the expense of Dallas. To accomplish this in 1936, with media attention focused on the $20 million Dallas exhibition, Carter needed something larger than life with the right man to pull it all together. A "livestock and frontier days exposition" did not even come close to what he had in mind. With the blessing of the local centennial committee, Carter put in a call to California, offering the job first to Rufus Le Maire, casting director of Metro-Goldwyn-Mayer. Le Maire, a native of New York, had grown up in Fort Worth but eventually returned to his birthplace to pursue a career as a theatrical agent. With the advent of sound movies, he transferred his base of operations to Hollywood as personal representative to actor George Arliss.[16] Le Maire rejected the assignment, but he told Carter of a producer currently in need of a show and promised to contact him.

Twenty years younger than Amon Carter and still in the formative stages of his career in 1936, Billy Rose craved notoriety. He was obsessed with it. He had owned several moderately successful nightclubs and produced a hit Broadway show, but these had not brought him lasting fame. So great was this need that he once hired an electric sign towering eighteen stories over Broadway to spell out just two words—"Billy Rose."[17] In the meantime, he smoldered impatiently in the shadow of his wife, Ziegfeld Follies star Fanny Brice. Broadway wags, behind his back, snidely dubbed him "Mr. Brice."

Rose had been raised in difficult circumstances. During a childhood of extreme poverty he learned early to scramble for a living. His family drifted through several New York City neighborhoods in the wake of his father, David Rosenberg, a Russian Jewish immigrant unable or unwilling to hold steady employment. His mother, Fanny, kept the family together. Forced to concentrate her energies on bringing in what money she could to support the family, she could spare little time for raising children. Left to fend for himself, Rose became adept at hustling meals, cigarettes, and pocket money on the streets and from sympathetic neighbors.

As he entered his teens, Rose knew he had to find a way to earn a more permanent living. With that end in mind, he enrolled in the Manhattan High School of Commerce. In 1914, school administrators selected a group of students, including Billy, to participate in testing a new system of shorthand devised by Irishman John Robert Gregg. Hoping eventually to sell the entire country on his system, Gregg opened an office in Manhattan and personally conducted many of the classes.

Under Gregg's tutelage, Rose emerged as a gifted student endowed with photographic recall and remarkable physical dexterity. Gregg sent his young protégé to a national business convention in 1916, where the teenager amazed tradesmen by taking high speed dictation with both hands simultaneously and then reading his untranscribed shorthand notes backward.[18] In January 1917

Rose led his high school team to the shorthand championship of New York State, writing 157 words per minute. On the night before the national competition, he went ice skating and fell, spraining his hand and wrist badly. The next day, instead of quitting the competition, Rose found a small potato he could grasp with his swollen hand, stuck a pen through it at a comfortable angle, and won the championship.[19] When the United States entered World War I, Rose's skill at both typing and shorthand brought him to the attention of Bernard Baruch, chairman of the War Industries Board. Baruch hired him for six months as his personal stenographer but, more importantly, became his friend and mentor, a role he continued to fill long after Rose attained prominence as the country's richest and most successful entertainment producer.

Following the war Rose again entered the employ of John Gregg, his mind now set on a steady if unglamorous office career. To increase his speed for stenography competitions, Rose began frequenting Keith's Vaudeville Theater, taking down the rapid fire routines in shorthand. This nightly exposure to the glamorous and highly competitive world of big-time vaudeville was a revelation to the impressionable teenager. Rose had no personal aspirations as a performer, but he discovered that even songwriters were making thousands of easy dollars by simply churning out formula lyrics. So great was the demand from the American public for new popular songs that Tin Pan Alley was born. The "Alley," a stretch of West Twenty-eighth Street between Broadway and Sixth Avenue, received its distinctive moniker from composer-lyricist Monroe Rosenfield, who noted in a series of articles for the *New York Herald* that the racket generated by competing piano players in the offices of various music publishers resembled tin pans being struck. In an era before readily available sound reproduction equipment, the demand for sheet music had helped musicians along the alley develop a booming industry. When the record industry began to market flat discs and the gramophone, the need for new song hits skyrocketed even higher. Between 1900 and 1910 alone, 100 songs had sheet music sales of one million even though the entire population of the United States at the time was less than ninety million. This simple statistic meant that even with several co-writers sharing the credit, there were still huge profits to be made.[20]

Rose abruptly scrapped his planned business career and began focusing the same word skills, concentration, and tenacity he had used in winning shorthand competitions to learning the art of songwriting. He studied the subjects, wording, and rhymes of past hits and struck up friendships with talented lyricists from whom he learned and with whom he frequently collaborated.[21] His first break came when a song he had written with Al Dubin and Joseph Meyer became the surprise showstopper of "Charlot's Revue of 1925," a musical starring Gertrude Lawrence. Over the next several years Rose shared the credits on a long string of popular hits including "You Tell Her, I Stutter," "Barney Google," "Me and My Shadow," "That Old Gang of Mine," "It's Only a Paper Moon," and "I Found a Million Dollar Baby in a Five and Ten Cent Store." He also claimed credit for the first singing commercial in America when Pepsi Cola adopted another tune of his, "Does the Spearmint Lose Its Flavor On the Bedpost Overnight?"[22]

While music scholars dispute many of Rose's contributions as a lyricist, his handsome share of the profits enabled him to open his first nightclub, the Backstage Club. The move also brought him out of the relative obscurity of Tin Pan Alley and one step closer to the pinnacle of show business success, Broadway. The Backstage Club was little more than a firetrap, but it attracted the interest of columnist Walter Winchell and Broadway notables who frequented the club scene. Among these celebrities was Ziegfeld Follies star Fanny Brice, recently divorced from gambler Nicky Arnstein. She and Rose married in 1929, attracted to each other more by mutual show business interests than any real passion; he was twenty-eight and she was thirty-six. Brice considered Rose stimulating and clever and found his sarcastic humor amusing; he evidently saw in her a powerful show business connection and believed such an alliance could advance his precarious career. Rose later dumped her unceremoniously in a very public affair with the glamorous and ambitious Eleanor Holm. Yet for years after the breakup of their marriage, Brice continued to insist she and Rose had never loved each other and that she had married Rose because she believed he could not hurt her.[23]

Despite a series of unprecedented flops, by the 1930s Rose had begun developing a unique production formula that evolved through the shows he produced over the next ten years. Like many Americans, he lamented the passing of vaudeville and believed that audiences would turn out to see a combination of slickly paced comedy, music, nostalgia, and burlesque. In 1933 Rose incorporated all these elements into the Casino de Paree, a nightclub-restaurant whose floor show featured Benny Goodman's jazz band, dancers Eleanor Powell and Bill "Bojangles" Robinson, and lots of chorus girls. Handsome "gigolos" wearing green carnations stood ready to dance with unescorted ladies or those just bored with their partners. In addition, Rose engaged a vaudeville agent to scour the country for eccentric acts that had never played New York. The acts selected by Rose for their quirkiness were a weird assortment. Packaged together as "The Small Time Revue," the complete bill featured such eclectic talents as Chaz Chase, "The Man Who Will Eat You Out of House and Home"; Eddie Eddy, the cry artist; a "Fat Girl Ballet;" and Andy Kennedy, playing jazz favorites on spoons. In between dining and the show, guests could dance on the stage.

Casino de Paree opened in December 1933 and soon was grossing $40,000 a week. Moving quickly to capitalize on the show's success, Rose opened a second theater within months: Billy Rose's Music Hall was meant to catch the overflow. For this new venture into planned nostalgia, he launched a second "Small Time Revue," hired 100 singing waiters to serenade the crowd, and projected the words to old silent movie songs on a screen so the audience could sing along. "The Lonely Hearts Club," 100 pretty girls in black satin dresses, stood by to entice unattached male customers onto the dance floor.[24]

There was only one problem with all this success. Rose, unable to raise capital on his own signature and unwilling to capitalize on his wife's name, had sought out gangsters to back his venture. The move was not that unusual, but unlike owners of other mob-backed clubs, he insisted on original music, top quality entertainers and relatively low prices. The strategy brought in plenty of business but cut heavily into profits. Rose's shadowy business partners began looking for ways to cut some of their losses. Rose unwittingly aided the maneuvering by choosing that moment in his career to take an extended vacation in Europe. His mob associates took advantage of his absence to get rid of some of their overhead. They cut staff, reduced service, fired many of the top acts, and raised prices. Upon his return, Rose confronted his gun-toting partners about violating their contract with him, dragging along columnist Walter Winchell as a reluctant witness. In a scene straight out of a B-grade gangster movie, one of his former associates reportedly informed Rose, "While you were in Europe, we shot out most of the clauses." Winchell told Rose he was in big trouble.[25]

Rose responded to the threat by abruptly cutting his losses, moving all the scenery and costumes to a secret location in New Jersey, and telephoning Bernard Baruch. Baruch placed a call to J. Edgar Hoover. Rose gave FBI agents names of the offending parties, a risky business itself, and within hours federal agents called on the mobsters advising them they could expect a government crackdown on all their operations if anything should happen to Rose. Rose took the precaution of hiring bodyguards, and he and Fanny ate all their meals at home for several months, but evidently the gangsters took the threat literally. No one ever attempted to molest him, and within weeks both Casino de Paree and the Music Hall closed down for good.[26]

Rose did not let the minor setback of death threats interfere long with a grandiose new plan he began concocting during his ill-timed European tour. Side trips to several indoor circuses and to a play about a circus romance had given him the germ of an idea. The entertainment he envisioned would require staging on a grand scale—too large to fit within the confines of the typical Broadway theater. The show would feature a romantic plot and musical production numbers set against the backdrop of a full indoor circus complete with aerialists, clowns, equestrian acts, lion tamers, elephants, and a human cannonball. The visibility afforded Rose by his recent club ventures helped him to solicit legitimate backing from a prominent young member of New York society, John Hay "Jock" Whitney.

Jock Whitney, a regular at Casino de Paree, who had earned his nickname playing polo, was part of a three-generation dynasty considered the aristocracy of American horse racing. Whitney himself had numerous show business interests and was heir to a family fortune estimated to be $100 million. His grandfather, William Collins Whitney, had amassed a huge fortune in street railways and served as secretary of the navy under President Grover Cleveland, and his mother was the daughter of John Hay, secretary of state under William McKinley and Theodore Roosevelt.[27] Whitney admired Billy Rose's track record for turning ideas into profit and agreed to bankroll his musical-circus venture.

With Whitney to insure a steady flow of cash, Rose began assembling an impressive production team. To create the music and lyrics, he enlisted Richard Rodgers and Lorenz Hart, while Ben Hecht and Charles MacArthur teamed to write the script. George Abbott agreed to direct; and John Murray Anderson, a veteran of the Greenwich Village Follies, Music Box Revue, and Ziegfeld Follies, signed on to do the complex staging of the large production numbers. Albert Johnson designed the scenery, and Raoul Pène duBois, the costumes. Charles MacArthur suggested calling the play appropriately, *Jumbo*, after P. T. Barnum's famous elephant.

To house the massive production, crews under the direction of Albert Johnson began gutting and renovating the Hippodrome Theater. Built in 1905, the Hippodrome established new standards for grand spectacle and lavish scenery in its heyday. The theater boasted a seating capacity of over 5,200, with standing room for 800 more. Built expressly to present major musical extravaganzas, the stage could hold a chorus of 500 and measured 110 feet deep by over 200 feet across.[28]

Jumbo opened in the Hippodrome on November 16, 1935, starring Jimmy Durante and also featuring Paul Whiteman and his jazz band, a negligible story line, and a complete circus. While the show ultimately lost money and ran for only 233 performances due to its enormous production costs, it played to over a million customers. More importantly, Rose's musicalized circus gamble won unanimous favor with the critics and achieved a type of immortality by virtue of one classic comic bit. Near the end of the first act, a police officer caught Durante in the obvious act of stealing an elephant.

"Where are you going with that elephant?" roared the cop.

Deadpanned Durante, "What elephant?"[29]

Jumbo did something else for Rose. The show established him as a producer of considerable organizational ability. If he himself could not write, act, choreograph, direct, orchestrate, sing, or dance, he knew who could. During the *Jumbo* period, Rose cemented the style that carried him on to eventual fame: circus bigness along the lines of the Ringling brothers and P. T. Barnum combined with the pageantry and glamour of a Ziegfeld Follies showcase.[30]

After receiving the urgent plea from Amon Carter in Texas, Rufus Le Maire tried for several days to contact Billy Rose in New York, but Rose, ironically, had left for California to join his wife. As Rose's fortunes on Broadway climbed steadily, Brice had begun building a new career in Hollywood. Rose wanted her to give up her career and retire, but Fanny liked Hollywood and proposed that Billy come west to explore the possibilities of becoming a movie producer. Fanny probably sensed correctly that unless she and Rose could move closer together artistically and geographically, their marriage was doomed.[31]

One afternoon, Rose took a shortcut across the courtyard of MGM's executive office building on his way to visit Fanny on the set of *The Great Ziegfeld*. Just as Rose strode past, Le Maire glanced out his second-story office window and spied the quarry he had sought in vain for days. He called down and within minutes had Rose in his office, attempting to explain to him why a producer with a reasonably promising Broadway career should abandon New York to produce a small, regional pioneer celebration 1,600 miles away. Rose had difficulty grasping the concept of the exposition: "It is the hundredth anniversary of the battle of the Alamo but it seems the Americans lost that battle. Why have a celebration?"[32]

Rose maintained his initial resistance for several days, evidently doubting Fort Worth's ability to raise the necessary capital. Amon Carter telegrammed *Jumbo* investor Jock Whitney, urging him to use his influence to persuade Rose to "drop over here to Fort Worth and give this project the once over." He assured Whitney that there would be no hesitation in the area of finances: "It will be an opportunity to make a substantial amount of money, well worth his time. With his genius and the financial backing we have there is no question of success."[33]

The arrival of Le Maire and Rose made local headlines in Fort Worth, but Rose remained coy with reporters about the reason for his stopover in Texas. He was here, he said, merely to scout possible sites for *Jumbo*, which he hoped to take on the road soon. He had just come from Hollywood where he discussed the sale of film rights to the same show.[34]

Planning committee members, led by Amon Carter, escorted Rose to the Frontier Days site and showed him a vacant pasture, remote from downtown and lacking even the most basic utilities. Rose had barely recovered from this shock before Carter cheerfully informed him that opening day was set for July 4th, only four months away. Later, over lunch at the Fort Worth Club, Rose probed the group's financial situation. Dallas, he learned, because of heavy investment by industrial exhibitors, could afford to sink $20 million into the official state exhibition. Fort Worth, thirty miles too far on the wrong fork of the Trinity, planned to spend only a paltry $500,000.

Rose requested a typewriter and a room to himself, and by three o'clock that afternoon hammered out several recommendations. But when he rejoined the committee the only livestock he mentioned had two legs and wore skirts:

> "There's only one thing that can compete with twenty million bucks of machinery, and that is girls—pelvic machinery. . . . We have to give them girls and more girls. Your only chance of bucking Dallas is entertainment on a grand scale, with a strong western flavor, but meeting big time standards in every way."[35]

After listening to tales about the sweltering heat of Texas summers, Rose warned against trying to compete during the day against the Dallas fair with its many acres of indoor exhibit space. He suggested instead a nighttime "cabaret fair," open only from 6:00 P.M. to 2:00 A.M. and run strictly for entertainment, because, he insisted, ". . . you haven't got any industrial exhibitors that amount to a damn anyway." He did allow that on Saturdays they could open a little earlier ". . . so the kiddies could come, not that we will have any attractions for children." Amon Carter spoke up. "In Texas the children are very precocious," he claimed.[36]

William Monnig, city councilman and president of the centennial board, displaying more restraint than the exuberant Carter, thought to ask how much all of this would cost. Rose estimated between $1 and $2 million, but he justified the high price tag:

You can't build what amounts to a small town and expect to amortize it in ninety days, which is how long your fair can expect to run. If you look at this fair as a business investment, you are sadly misguided. But if you look at it as a venture in civic exploitation, it will pay big dividends in the long run. Some of the shows will show a profit on their dollars. . . . And if it's consolation to you . . . Dallas will be losing twenty million.[37]

Several committee members objected, but Amon Carter insisted, "Nothing is too big for the state of Texas." Monnig, the voice of caution, asked Rose about his fee. Rose did not mince words, "I would like a flat $100,000."

"That's a lot of money," said Monnig.

"That's right, replied Rose, "but this involves a lot of work."[38]

The committee asked Rose to leave the room while they discussed his proposal and voted. Ten minutes later Carter emerged to tell him he had a deal; even then Rose needed further prodding from Jock Whitney and the additional guarantee of a $25,000 advance before he agreed. On March 7 he signed, persuaded no doubt by the rather remarkable Depression-era salary of $100,000 for only 100 days' work.[39] The bargain was personally guaranteed by Amon Carter. On his way out of town, Rose sent an urgent cable to Paris, where his chief *Jumbo* director, John Murray Anderson, was vacationing. "Have interesting job in Fort Worth, Texas. Can you leave immediately?"

"Have left," wired Anderson.[40]

Rose later called the decision by Rufus Le Maire to recommend him to the Fort Worth Fiesta planners a turning point in his career, one of several important stepping stones by which he moved from the ranks of local producer to the status of national celebrity.

"WE'LL GIVE 'EM A BOLT... A BALL OF FIRE"

n July 9, 1936, the *Fort Worth Press* jubilantly proclaimed, "Fort Worth Now Is the Army of *Employed*," a headline accurately reflecting the enormous impact of the centennial on the economy of Fort Worth. The inauguration of two major construction projects—the Will Rogers complex and now the Frontier Centennial—brought a much-needed lift to the spirits of the community and guaranteed that at least 1,500 Texans, 1,200 of them from Fort Worth, would no longer be out of work.[1] The fortunate recipients of those jobs filled a wide variety of positions that ranged from dancers and showgirls to electricians, carpenters, cashiers, ticket sellers, gatemen, cooks, waiters, busboys, porters, dishwashers, and cigarette and hat-check girls.

Although Fort Worth had not been as hard hit by the Depression as some communities, by the mid-thirties many men who later went on to earn college degrees had been reduced to such menial tasks as raking leaves in city parks or sweeping out restaurants for a few dollars a week in order to survive. A major building program already under way—a tuberculosis sanatorium, sewage disposal plant, as well as other jobs created by the PWA and the Works Progress Administration (WPA)—had delayed the major effects of the crash, but on November 30, 1932, the Fort Worth City Council moved to appropriate $100 a month for operation of a soup kitchen. Although business would begin to recover by the late thirties, in 1936 this had yet to occur. Announcement of the new construction came as a godsend.[2]

Groundbreaking ceremonies
inaugurate construction of the
Frontier Centennial Celebration
Will Rogers Memorial Complex,
March 10, 1936. Wielding gilt
shovels are *Star-Telegram*
owner/publisher, Amon Carter;
Fort Worth Mayor Van Zandt
Jarvis; P.W.A. Chief Engineer
Uel Stephens; and Centennial
Board President William Monnig.

Courtesy Fort Worth Star-Telegram
Photographic Collection, Photographic
Archives, Special Collections, University
of Texas at Arlington Library.
Hereinafter, Special Collections, UTA.

Fort Worth advertising executive and historian William E. Jary, Jr., later declared, "The advance promo on the Fort Worth Centennial must go down in history books as the wildest ever."[3] Billy Rose had little experience in the subtleties of agrarian pride and partriotic fervor. With the finalizing of contracts, he guilelessly launched a campaign of tub-thumping flummery in the local press, glibly side-stepping references to struggling pioneers, martyred patriots and epic struggles for freedom. Rose's condensed version of events skipped the war and got straight to the victory party. He announced plans for "a mammoth open air dance floor accommodating 3,000 couples, singing waiters, a giant screen flashing the words of popular tunes for mass sing songs." Rose proclaimed, "The Fort Worth show will bring 5,000,000 visitors. . . . It should gross $2 million—no, it'll be a five million dollar show!" Answering reporters' queries of how he planned to accomplish such a feat, Rose replied, "We'll give 'em a bolt . . . a ball of fire. . . . Let Dallas . . . educate the people. . . . We'll entertain them in Fort Worth." Rose dismissed concerns over similar expositions that had featured girlie shows and nudity to draw in customers, saying, "Nine persons out of ten are revolted by smut. It has no place in show business."[4]

His capacity for exaggeration seemed limitless. He dropped the names of top headliners such as George Burns and Gracie Allen, Jack Benny, Shirley Temple, Dick Powell, Clark Gable, and Phil Baker. Backing these, he promised, would be a chorus of 500 beautiful girls. Rose sold Fort Worth with the spurious zeal of a con artist. The bravado of his statements to reporters served chiefly to divert attention from the facts—as yet he had formulated no definite plans or concept for the show.

A few days after signing to produce the show, Rose returned to New York City where he held a press conference in the Hippodrome Theater, focusing attention on the still unnamed Fort Worth exposition. As stagehands dismantled scenery around him, Rose climbed atop a packing crate to announce that he would close down *Jumbo* immediately and move it—all two hundred performers—to the wilds of "West Texas." He intended to charter a special train for the move, "with, of course, a baggage car for Jimmy Durante's schnozzle." Rose evidently made the latter statement without consulting Durante, because shortly he announced that the popular comedian would not make the trip to Texas after all.[5]

The press conference focused on Rose's new extravaganza. "The exposition in Dallas will show the progress of art, education and culture during the last 100 years," he lectured, "but my exposition will show just the opposite if possible." Reporters seemed mystified by the need for two Texas centennial celebrations. New York columnist Lucius Beebe assured his readers that the eccentric rivalry between the neighboring cities could best be understood as ". . . intramural genealogical exchanges and slats-pasting of an epic order . . . between Amon Carter, first citizen of Fort Worth, and the harassed and slightly terrified city fathers of Dallas."[6]

Rose continued shamelessly to embellish his earlier pronouncements. "I'm going to put on a show the likes of which has never before been seen by the human eye. I am offering many famous artists bags of gold to join us and many will surely succumb to my blandishments," he asserted. "I'll get Shirley Temple, Mae West, Guy Lombardo, Jack Benny. . . . I'll get 1,000 beautiful girls for the 'Frontier Follies.' Then I'll have a Texas pageant to be called 'The Fall of the Alamo,' 'The Battle of San Jacinto' or some other Texas name. I'll have 2,000 Indians and 1,000 cowboys and guess who wins. I'll make *Jumbo* look like a peep show."[7]

In his initial statements to reporters Rose maintained, "Only twice in amusement history has the public responded to smut. That was Little Egypt in 1893 and Sally Rand at the Century of Progress (a reference to the 1933 Chicago World's Fair). We don't need any fans or bubble dancers at the Texas Frontier Centennial, and we won't have them."[8] In New York, Rose backed away from his original statement: "I am supposed to keep it clean," he admitted, but "the show will probably be a little on the nude side. Sally Rand stopped off and spent a couple of days—make that a couple of hours—with me, and I offered a big piece of change to show her charms to me and my fellow Texans."[9] Billy had begun referring to himself as a native, though it never became clear who conferred citizenship or when.

Rose concluded the press conference by proclaiming to reporters that he was severely underpaid and let drop that Texans considered him "kind of a genius."[10] New York, like Fort Worth, tried to make sense of it all, confused by the peculiar mix of Texas history and show business glitz.

By late March, Rose was back in Fort Worth, ensconced in an office in the downtown Sinclair Building on the corner of Fifth and Main streets. Amon Carter concentrated his energies on raising the necessary operating cash, leaving day-to-day show preparations entirely to Rose, although the two stayed in close contact. In addition to his $100,000 salary, the show business trade publication *Variety* reported Rose had at his disposal $50,000 for the hiring of his own administrative staff and an additional $150,000 for the purchasing of topflight "name" talent.[11] This did not stop Rose from fretting to Carter about a variety of problems ranging from the opening of his personal mail to stock show manager John B. Davis' request that Rose dispense with personal salutations on telegrams because these added additional charges. He grumbled, "I am down here in Fort Worth solely through your good offices. . . . There's too much for all of us to do to worry about this kind of niggeldy-piggeldy saving of pennies. My time is costing the Centennial too much for me to be harrassed or hampered—let alone embarrassed." Carter also fielded some of Rose's ideas for publicity stunts, including one suggestion to petition Adolph Hitler for loan of the Zeppelin to transport fifty showgirls from New York to Texas, and another to request Lord Rothermere to ship a baby elephant aboard the luxury liner, *Queen Mary*.[12]

Rose continued to shuttle between Texas and New York via eleven-hour plane flights twice weekly, often putting in twenty-hour workdays. Exercising his newly acquired power as director general, he scrapped plans for most of the original buildings as well as the exposition's original concept of a historical pageant. Contradicting himself again, he told members of the Junior Chamber of Commerce, "We'll have no pageants in the Fort Worth centennial. I've slept through so many of those things I'm convinced they're financed by the aspirin people." The new version would revolve around the theme, "Texas Under Six Flags" and would include a pioneer village as well as the "Frontier Follies," described naively by Rose as a "musicalized rodeo."[13]

Rose officially inaugurated the advertising campaign on March 14, 1936, by taking out advertisements in two show business trade publications—*Billboard* and *Variety*. The ads proclaimed, "In the words of John Mason Brown of the *New York Post*, 'Billy Rose has wrapped the voluminous cloak of P. T. Barnum around his shoulders.' And with his cooperation, Fort Worth will offer to America, not a pale carbon copy of the Chicago World's Fair, but a Living, Breathing, Highly Exciting Version of The Last Frontier."[14] The ads drew the ire of Arthur L. Kramer, a member of the management committee of the Dallas centennial, who complained to Fort Worth centennial board President William Monnig. Claiming that the intent of the ads was to malign Dallas, Kramer threatened, "the Dallas exposition has the right to demand that no other city in Texas refer to it either directly or by implication in any advertisement or publicity relating to a competitive attraction. It becomes our responsibility to protect this right. . . ." In his reply to Kramer, Monnig was unapologetic: "I have had the old-fashioned idea that Texas, or even the centennial, does not belong to any one city. I should regret to have you feel that the Fort Worth Frontier Centennial must ask your approval of our program. . . . We must reserve the right . . . to publicize it in the manner best calculated, in our judgment to achieve the desired ends."[15] *Variety*, alerted to the growing tussle, helped to add further fuel to the anger of Dallas civic leaders by reporting, "Now little Fort Worth, its local pride restored, wahooes over to great big Dallas, 'Ft. Worth, the Last Frontier!' it yippees, 'and Billy Rose is our prophet!' Says Dallas . . . 'Why, that little cow town! Billy Rose, what kind of a cowboy is he?' Humph, harumph, and stuff!"[16]

The hodgepodge of talent that descended on Fort Worth in the wake of the ads might have daunted a man of more refined sensibilities, but Rose evidently perceived opportunity in such diverse applicants as a man who claimed to be Jesse James and had documents to prove it; Bozo, Ripley's Wonder Dog "Who Reads the Mind"; something called a "bubble illusion" show; and magician Hardeen Houdini, Harry's younger brother. Rose hired them all. The centennial also could boast of the "world's largest steer," a longhorn modestly described as standing six feet, two inches in height, and over twelve feet long from nose to tail.

One applicant the same height as Rose failed to make the cut (Rose stood barely five feet, two inches, tall but habitually wore shoes designed to make him appear taller).

"What do you do?" Rose asked him.

"I'm a midget," the man replied.[17]

Contributing to the already surrealistic atmosphere of the proceedings came Joe Peanuts and his Simian Gigolos, an eight-piece monkey band, hired evidently in the interest of culture. C. J. Maxwell walked into the centennial offices one day and dumped the contents of his briefcase—a two-headed snake—onto Rose's desk. Rose retreated hastily to a far corner of the room but later boasted to reporters of his chilling encounter with a rattlesnake. True to form, he strayed from the facts. The deadly "rattler" was nothing more than a harmless bull snake.[18]

In his New York clubs Rose had on several occasions employed "gigolos" as dance partners for unaccompanied women. He repeated the strategy by advertising in the *New York Herald Tribune* and other major newspapers seeking "100 bona fide noblemen whose titles stem from either active or extinct monarchies, and who, for adventurous or economic reasons, are willing to serve as dancing partners for the flower of Texas." The advertised salary was $100 a week. Applicants had to meet rigid qualifications and submit proof of ancestry. "Bogus counts," warned the ad, "masqueraders and descendants of the Dauphin will get short shrift."[19] Like so many of his other grandiose claims, the blue bloods failed to materialize, and eventually most observers dismissed the claim as another of Rose's publicity stunts. However, three local promoters—Ed Beck, John O. Flautt, and David Smith—figured to upstage Rose by wiring Emperor Haile Selassie of Ethiopia and offering him $100,000 to appear at the centennial. Selassie did not bother to reply, and for their trouble the three entrepreneurs found themselves stuck with a cable bill totaling $24.84.[20]

By early April bids had been opened and contracts assigned. The lucrative design contract for the main open-air pavilion and other structures went to the architectural firm of Joseph R. Pelich. Actual construction of the outdoor amphitheater was to be carried out by three local firms—Harry Friedman, James T. Taylor, and Thomas Byrne.[21] A small army of laborers moved in immediately to begin the task of transforming neglected, vacant land into the showcase envisioned by Billy Rose, all within a matter of weeks. Workers first concentrated on the major structures of the exhibition—a 2,800-seat circular building modeled after European indoor circuses and designed to house *Jumbo*; an outdoor pavilion for a rodeo-Wild West pageant called "The Last Frontier," and a 4,000-seat outdoor cafe-amphitheater to house the exhibition's centerpiece, the "Frontier Follies."

The proposed amphitheater possessed a number of unique architectural features, including the world's largest revolving stage—130 feet in diameter and weighing 17,000 tons. The engineering for this "leviathan of rostrums," as advertising styled it, was designed by Richard Bruckner, a Russian immigrant who had previously engineered the equipment for *Jumbo*. A complete revolution of the stage required one minute and forty-five seconds. The stage itself rested on metal tracks in a tank of water nine feet deep, making the stage appear to "float" toward or away from the audience. One 450-horsepower motor controlled the revolutions of the stage, and another, equally powerful, "floated" the stage forward and backward on its submerged tracks. The lagoon created for this man-made "island" measured 130 feet by 175 feet. Canals leading to the pool opened with drawbridges and ended in large turning basins. Forty-three pipes mounted on the front rim of the lagoon shot geysers of water into the air at strategic intervals to provide a curtain effect; an additional twenty-one fountains rested on the bottom of the pool waiting to be hand-levered into position by stagehands after the stage slid backward. The central structure of the revolving stage, combining a permanent theatrical set, twin bandstands, and dressing rooms located beneath, weighed 4,364,000 pounds, necessitating the gargantuan motors required to move it.[22]

The actual building was as impressive in scale as its stage. Over thirty blue-and-white Spanish-style arches, each rising nearly thirty feet to the roof, stretched 280 feet around the curve of the building's 320-foot frontal façade. The sheltered area supported by the arches protected two levels of horseshoe boxes and a fifty-foot bar billed as the world's longest. Theater patrons arrived through the covered outer façade bordering the entrance to the theater and emerged again into the open air on the other side. Before them nineteen graduated tiers of seating spread out in a wide fan and descended to the water-filled lagoon and stage at the lowest level. Tables placed on each of the fan-shaped tiers permitted theater customers to dine in comfort while viewing the show. Double tiers of smaller arches completely framed the perimeter of the outdoor seating area and extended to the permanent stage setting as well, continuing the design of the massive entryway.[23]

Other major attractions also began to take shape, laid out along a broad, w-shaped promenade. Prominent among these was an exact reproduction of Will Roger's Santa Monica, California, ranch house living room, a tribute to Amon Carter's longstanding friendship with the humorist. For the occasion, the Rogers family loaned personal articles and memorabilia in the room, including trophies, saddles, spurs, quirts, oil paintings, and furniture. The exhibit was placed inside the West Texas Chamber of Commerce building, a replica of a

Aerial view of the Fort Worth Centennial Exposition. Clockwise from the upper left, major buildings of the Exposition are Casa Mañana, The Last Frontier, Pioneer Palace, Jumbo, and The Sunset Trail at the bottom. Present-day University Drive is on the extreme left.

Courtesy Special Collections, UTA.

western train station. On the first leg of the 'w' the Sunset Trail recreated a frontier western street with a church, a fully equipped working blacksmith shop, the Silver Dollar Dance Hall, the *Daily Star* newspaper office, the Astor Hotel and a replica of the saloon of Judge Roy Bean, Law West of the Pecos. Rose placed the historical exhibits just inside the main gate facing Camp Bowie Boulevard "so that the public can get through them first and have it over with, and then be free to have fun with a clear historical conscience."[24] So reported roving Scripps-Howard columnist Ernie Pyle.

Rose had final say on every aspect of every exhibit and clashed on several occasions with women's organizations who disagreed with his ideas on how to present a decorously wholesome and patriotic picture of Texas life for out-of-state visitors. At one point Rose banished an heirloom set of lace curtains hung in a Gay Nineties room, calling them "too frilly" for the rustic exteriors of the Sunset Trail. On another day, Edith Alderman Guedry, the prim society editor of the *Fort Worth Press*, reported that Rose had shocked the ladies by proclaiming that a certain museum exhibit looked like "hell and a bunch of spinach."[25]

While supposedly targeting a broad cross section of the general public, major centennial attractions leaned prominently in concept toward Fort Worth's Wild West heritage. The Pioneer Palace featured a large dance floor and a forty-foot western-style bar. An elevated stage remained hidden until just before showtime when three large mirrors over the bar rolled backward on their wooden framework, like garage doors, to reveal the saloon-girl chorus line. A replica of a stockaded frontier fort went up on the corner of Montgomery Street and Crestline Drive. From it, the Black Horse Troop of the Second United States Cavalry, dressed in authentic uniforms of nineteenth-century Texas Dragoons, was scheduled to give daily equestrian demonstrations. To make the costumes accurate, actual uniforms had to be borrowed from the Smithsonian Institution at a cost of $5,000 because, ironically, none could be found in Texas.[26] Additional attractions included a midway, where Rose intended to feature several burlesque shows, and a "monkey mountain." The fifty-foot mountain, placed in the center of a man-made island surrounded by a water-filled moat, would house 180 monkeys from the Fort Worth Zoo. Architects sagely assured Rose that the island's simian inhabitants could not escape across the ditch.

If Billy Rose was not universally well known in 1936, he was rapidly developing a reputation for his ability to organize a show much larger than his own diminutive stature. This unique talent enabled him to attract some of the most talented writers, designers, and technicians of the New York theater community for *Jumbo*. This same staff, virtually intact, followed Rose to Texas. The list included stage director John Murray Anderson; scenic designer Albert Johnson; choreographers Robert Alton and Lauretta Jefferson; technical designer Carlton Winckler; and costume designer Raoul Pène du Bois.

John Murray Anderson, stage director for all shows connected with the Frontier Centennial, had produced some of the leading musicals of the 1920s and had directed both the Ziegfeld Follies and Paul Whiteman's movie, *The King of Jazz*, the first full-color motion picture. Anderson's formula was always the same: a slender story line, comedy, escapism, and lots of beautiful girls and visual splendor. Anderson and Rose had the same eye for expansive and glittery pageantry, but, unlike Rose, Anderson also had the ability to realize his visions in terms of color, design, choreography, and story.[27]

No two men were less alike. Anderson, the calm at the eye of the storm, was cultured and serious, every inch the gentleman. Rose, on the other hand, was brash, getting his way mainly through bluster. As Rose's reputation as a producer grew, Anderson, the man actually executing those dreams, tended to be forgotten. Nevertheless, he stayed with Rose for two decades following the Texas Centennial, evidently because Rose allowed him full and free artistic expression. Anderson himself later admitted in his autobiography that despite the "tough guy" image Rose liked to present, he never broke a contract and often far exceeded the terms agreed upon. An artistic bond, rather than one of friendship, held two very opposite personalities together.[28]

Anderson's directing style mixed wit and sarcasm in equal doses, a lethal combination that became legendary in theatrical circles. Watching an Anderson rehearsal became a favorite pastime for newsmen assigned to cover the goings-on. At one of the centennial's early practice sessions, Anderson tested the resolve of the dancers and showgirls when he witheringly proclaimed, "We have too many of you wretched girls anyway, so if a single one of you makes one sound you'll automatically be thrown out."[29]

This sardonic tendency manifested itself further in the bewildering cornucopia of nicknames that Anderson routinely bestowed on his charges, seeming to prefer these to the drudgery of recalling conventional surnames. Each nickname reflected some personality quirk or physical trait of the performer. Names such as Amarillo, Stooge, Butch, Dry Ice, Goo-Goo, the Eyebrow Sisters, Mona Lisa, and Chigger were routine. Even staff members were not immune. The youthful Raoul Pène du Bois became "One More Spring," while Albert Johnson was dubbed "Sandwich," reflecting a propensity to consume a dozen or more chicken sandwiches every day. Rose became the "Mad Hatter," a title well suited to his role as frenetic overseer of the organized mayhem swirling around the opening preparations. But perhaps the best known moniker belonged to "Stuttering Sam," Anderson's name for Mary Dowell, the daughter of Fort Worth's captain of detectives (later police chief), A. E. Dowell. The speech impediment that earned Dowell her sobriquet also proved to be one of her most endearing assets. Dowell had approached Rose initially on behalf of her sister Virginia, believing herself too awkward for a spot in the show. Her ingenuous innocence impressed Rose to the extent that he hired both sisters as showgirls. Following the run of the centennial, Mary Dowell, a statuesque redhead over six feet tall, went on with Rose to New York City, where she continued as one of his top showgirls.

A penchant for nicknames was not John Murray Anderson's only idiosyncrasy. Once rehearsals had begun, the director never changed his suit no matter how threadbare or ragged it might become. Only when the show had opened successfully would he change; he then burned the rehearsal suit ceremonially.[30]

Technical director for the centennial's shows was twenty-eight-year-old lighting specialist Carlton Winckler. Other engineers had warned Rose that focused light throws would be impossible in the outdoor cabaret theater, where distances as great as 200 feet separated the stage from lighting equipment. Winckler solved the problem by placing glass reflectors ground like lenses behind 1,500 incandescent lamps, thereby concentrating the light for the required distance. Operating the switchboards for the array required twelve electricans during each show.[31]

The scenic designer for the Frontier Centennial had also worked with both Anderson and Rose. Rose had previously assigned "Sandwich" Johnson the chore of transforming New York's Hippodrome Theater for *Jumbo*, and in Fort Worth he expected the same metamorphosis. Johnson set to work designing not only the sets of the Frontier Follies, but all other sets, buildings, and concessions for the entire Frontier Centennial. He was well prepared for the task, having produced over fifty shows as artistic director of Radio City Music Hall in addition to

designing for such notables of the theater as vaudeville mogul Lee Shubert and the Ben Hecht-Charles MacArthur team in their movies *Crime Without Passion* and *The Scoundrel*.[32]

Costume design for all the shows of the exhibition was done by Raoul Pène du Bois, who at the age of twenty-four already had to his credit both Radio City Music Hall and the 1934 Ziegfeld Follies. After Fort Worth, du Bois continued in an illustrious career designing costumes and sets for countless Broadway shows including *Call Me Madam*, *DuBarry Was a Lady*, *Leave It to Me* (the musical in which Texan Mary Martin made her Broadway debut), *Too Many Girls*, *Bells Are Ringing*, *Gypsy*, and *The Music Man*.[33]

From left to right, dance director Robert Alton, technical and lighting director Carlton Winckler and stage director John Murray Anderson.

Courtesy Special Collections, UTA.

Twenty-four-year old Raoul Pène du Bois, costume designer for both the Frontier Centennial and Frontier Fiesta.

Courtesy Special Collections, UTA.

Dance director was Robert Alton, and the musical numbers for the show were all written by twenty-one-year-old Dana Suesse. Equally at home with both classical and popular music, Suesse had debuted her "Waltz Rhapsody" at Carnegie Hall when she was only seventeen. She also had several popular hits to her credit, including "You Ought To Be In Pictures," introduced in the 1934 Ziegfeld Follies by Jane Froman, and "Whistling In the Dark."[34] One of her tunes, "The Night Is Young and You're So Beautiful," was later recorded by several artists including Bing Crosby and Mario Lanza and became so popular with crowds during the summer of 1936 that Rose adopted it as the unofficial theme song of the Frontier Centennial.

Suesse supposedly composed the tune in one improbable late-night session after Billy Rose and John Murray Anderson, stuck for a big number in a particular scene, roused her from a sound sleep in a downtown hotel. Disconcerted, without makeup and wearing curlers, she grudgingly admitted the two to her suite, complaining of the late hour. Rose berated her lack of enthusiasm, saying, "The night is young." Noting her obvious discomposure, Anderson then added dryly, "And you're so beautiful." With such improbable inspiration, Suesse proceeded to the piano in her sitting room and completed "The Night Is Young and You're So Beautiful" in a little over an hour. Presumably she then returned to bed.[35]

To complete his staff, Rose named local musician Hyman Maurice to serve as musical director for all shows. Maurice, a product of the Warsaw Conservatory, had immigrated to the United States following World War I after touring as a member of the Russian Symphony. In the United States he joined the Publix Theater Circuit as John Murray Anderson was assembling the first show sent out over the circuit. In 1927 when Publix opened the Worth Theater, Maurice came to Fort Worth as orchestra director and remained to make the city his home even after the Worth abandoned weekly shows.[36]

To handle the staggering task of creating the estimated 2,000 costumes needed for the entire centennial, Rose engaged Brooks Costumes, one of New York City's oldest and most respected theatrical firms. Rather than tackling the job from its New York base, Brooks opened a construction shop on the fifth floor of Monnig's Wholesale Warehouse, 1619 Main Street, next to the present-day Water Gardens. The company bolstered its own imported staff with 150 local seamstresses. Personally supervising the preparations was A. M. Blumberg, Brooks' general manager. Fittings, lasting all day for the more elaborate costumes, were convenient because Rose also scheduled rehearsals for the warehouse.[37]

Although the name Frontier Centennial stuck, by late spring the amphitheater housing the Frontier Follies had acquired a shiny new title—Casa Mañana,

Frontal facade of Casa Mañana as the cabaret theater nears completion in the summer of 1936.

Courtesy Special Collections, UTA.

the House of Tomorrow—because, Rose proclaimed, the outdoor cabaret theater would be "100 light years ahead of anything like it yet built." Originally Rose had planned to call the new showplace Casa Diablo, House of the Devil, but John Murray Anderson suggested Casa Mañana, calling the latter more appropriate to the atmosphere of the celebration. Behind the scenes, the name change temporarily wrought havoc because the printing of nearly 500,000 advertising posters and brochures with Casa Diablo had already begun.[38]

With the machinery of production finally in place and operational in late March, Rose took the next step, announcing open auditions for dancers and showgirls. He was emphatic that dancing talent was not enough, declaring to reporters, "There won't be a woman in the Fort Worth show who isn't a looker."[39] The added lure of $25 dollars a week, in an era when men worked for as little as $12.50, resulted in a deluge of applicants that caught even Rose off guard. Several thousand star-struck applicants, aspiring actresses, and stage mothers dragging their tap-dancing teenage daughters descended on Fort Worth. Some had traveled hundreds of miles, coming even from surrounding states, all just for a chance at a spot in the chorus.

Preliminary auditions for showgirls were held first at the North Side Coliseum and later moved to the Hotel Texas as less suitable applicants were eliminated. Rose shouted for quiet, threatening to send everyone home if he didn't get it. Most were sent packing unceremoniously anyway, failing to survive even the first cut. Dismissing one candidate, he advised her, "Ask Mama to spend more money on your dancing lessons." With another he was even more blunt: "Not in a million years—sorry." After witnessing the scene, *Press* amusements reporter Jack Gordon concluded, "The ones [Rose] liked may go into his Frontier Follies. The others we imagine will go out and round up their big brothers."[40]

One of the survivors, Janice Nicolson, recalled later, "I didn't particularly want to do it—my mother shooed me down, me and my sister. All of our friends that danced were going. We'd do a few time steps just to see if we could dance . . . and [Rose] wanted us to do kicks. Then they would eliminate." Anderson and Rose told the most attractive girls, including Nicolson and her sister, Olive, that they would be contacted about starting rehearsals.[41]

One girl who traveled the short distance from Weatherford, Texas, to try out was quickly disqualified, partly because of her interest in feature billing. Wearing a top hat and a little cutaway tuxedo, she sang and performed a specialty number to the tune "Gloomy Sunday," backed by the Marionettes, a group of students from her own dancing studio. Beth Lea, who eventually won a spot in the revue as a showgirl witnessed the scene:

> When she finished, Billy Rose told her that she was very, very good, but he just did not have a place for her in the show. He said, "You're not good enough for a spot, but you're too good for the chorus." The girls that were trying out—we gave her the biggest hand. She's the only one I saw that the

people broke out into applause. We listened to her and she projected. Someone might have beat her at some kind of dancing, but she had star quality—it was there.[42]

Rose, unimpressed, informed her, "I am not running an amateur show—come back when you make a name for yourself." Still, he offered the girl and her pupils spots in the chorus. Two of the dancers, sisters Marzelle and Margie Van Hoosier, accepted. Their teacher, the star of the act, turned down the offer to follow at least part of Rose's advice. Two years later, while in New York City attending the debut of Cole Porter's *Leave It To Me*, John Murray Anderson noticed the same girl featured in a show-stopping song-and-dance number. He looked up her name in the program. The girl he and Rose had rejected as hayseed talent was Mary Martin, and the number she was singing, "My Heart Belongs To Daddy," became her trademark.[43]

The dancers and showgirls eventually assigned spots in the Casa Mañana Revue came from diverse backgrounds and brought with them a variety of youthful ambitions. For many the experience was a lark, an exhilarating brush with the perceived glamour of show business. For other performers, like Beth Lea of Fort Worth, appearing in the Casa Mañana line held a different allure—providing a means to earn money toward such impossible luxuries as a college education in difficult economic times. Many, too young even to sign their own contracts, had to have their parents sign for them.[44] Performing in the centennial became, literally, a family affair for some of the youthful chorus members. Sixteen-year-old Elizabeth Morris trekked over 300 miles from Amarillo, won a place in the show during preliminary auditions, and then wrote her big sister Jean to come and audition also. Local dancers simply lived at home, while out-of-town performers found rooms together or boarded with relatives who often doubled as chaperones. The lure of performing in such an exotic setting as Casa Mañana sometimes led to comical situations. When John Murray Anderson advised showgirls to send their boyfriends around to apply for jobs as gondoliers and showboys, he underestimated the determination of some applicants. J. D. Farmer of Fort Worth sidestepped possible competitors by rousing the bleary-eyed director shortly after dawn one morning with the pronouncement that "the boatman" had arrived.

Opportunism abounded even among those who had no interest in performing. Teenagers Charlie Tandy and Phil North, son of *Star-Telegram* editor James M. North, learned that one planned number required fifty-six pairs of gold-painted cowboy boots—enough for all the showgirls and dancers. Tandy's father owned a leather store and sold dyes and other shoe repair equipment wholesale, and the two contracted with Rose to re-gild the boots. Each night five girls were given time off. Tandy and North would arrive at the centennial grounds, pick up the five pairs of boots, stay to see the show, take the boots home to Tandy's garage for repainting, then repeat the process the next night. As they waited between shows, the teens lingered in the Pioneer Palace, where they observed that gamblers at the slot machines often gave up after failing to win a payoff after several tries. The pair would then commandeer the abandoned machine, invest a dime or two from their pooled pocket change, and as often as not earn back their investment with a dollar jackpot. As soon as they "hit," they would quit for the night.[45]

The dancing auditions still did not produce talent in quantities sufficient to please Rose. To remedy the situation he announced that 100 experienced dancers and showgirls would be imported from New York to bolster the ranks of local talent. He also declared a statewide search for "Texas' most beautiful females," with the search to culminate in a pageant to select "Texas Sweetheart Number One." The contest, held at Fort Worth's Central High School auditorium on May 30, drew contestants from seventy-five Texas cities with the double inducement of a six-month movie contract for the winner and a chance to appear in the Casa Mañana Revue. Rose himself judged the contest, aided by John Murray Anderson, nationally syndicated New York columnist Lucius Beebe, and Dr. Webb Walker, a local physician. To inspire the judges, Ed Lally's orchestra struck up "The Most Beautiful Girl in the World," taken appropriately from Rose's own show *Jumbo*.

After the panel had narrowed the field to three, Rose led each girl forward, encouraging audience members to applaud their choice of the prettiest. Still, when it came to the final decision, Rose ignored the popular favorite and selected Faye Cotton, a cafe cashier from Borger. One local amusements

Billy Rose and beauty queen hopefuls from across the state take to the stage of Central High School Auditorium on May 30, 1936, in a contest to choose "Texas Sweetheart Number One."

Courtesy Fort Worth Public Library.

columnist characterized the winner as "fresh as the daisy fields and charming for her sweetness and poise." Cotton had entered the Fort Worth contest literally by chance—she and the only other aspirant flipped a coin to determine who would represent the small Panhandle town.[46] She was so convinced that she had no chance in the competition that she arrived in Fort Worth with only one change of clothing.

At about the same time, the Dallas exposition was conducting its own beauty contest to select a "Texas Bluebonnet Girl." The competing pageants were only one indication, however, that the publicity war between Fort Worth and Dallas was heating up. While Dallas solemnized the historical and cultural glories of the main celebration, signs and billboards began appearing all over Texas and several surrounding states proclaiming, *"Fort Worth For Entertainment; Dallas For Education."* For those missing the point, the posters featured a smiling, scantily clad cowgirl who waved enticingly from astride a bucking horse.[47]

The bond subscription committee, under the leadership of Amon Carter, redoubled efforts to raise the $750,000 needed to complete the centennial showgrounds. To aid in the effort, the official advertising brochure of the Frontier Centennial began circulating widely. It proclaimed,

Unquestionably the House of Tomorrow . . . not only a Day, but a Decade in Advance of its Times. . . . The Largest Cafe-Theater Ever Constructed. . . . Tables and Chairs for 4500 Amusement Lovers . . . A Gargantuan Revolving-Reciprocating Stage . . . Three and a Half Times Larger than that of Radio City Music Hall . . . Two 450 h.p. Motors Required to Operate this Leviathan of Rostrums, with its Lovely Freight of 250 Eye-Bedeviling Coryphees over a Pool of Limpid Crystal containing 617,000 Gallons of Real Water . . . SPECTACLE and SONG, DANCE and COM-EDY . . . Past Peradventure the BIGGEST GIRL SHOW EVER PRO-DUCED . . . Star-Studded with FOREMOST CELEBRITIES OF STAGE, SCREEN and RADIO.[48]

Beneath the text of the ad ran a picture supposedly depicting the stage show, featuring several of the "eye-bedeviling coryphees" frolicking topless in

Aerial view of Casa Mañana. Present-day University Drive can be seen at bottom of photograph.

Courtesy Special Collections, UTA.

Casa Mañana's lagoon. This was a complete fabrication, existing only in the artfully puerile imagination of Ned Alvord, Billy Rose's eccentric press agent. Well known in show business circles, Alvord had earned the title "the deacon" for his habit of wearing a cutaway frock coat, wing collar, tortoise-rimmed spectacles, and a derby hat. For his sojourn in Fort Worth's simmering heat, he had a seersucker "tuxedo" specially tailored. Rose, unsure how locals might respond to Alvord, confided to reporters, "Alvord looks like a deacon but does not talk like one."[49] Nor did he behave like one. One of Alvord's favorite ploys was to drop in at the composing room of a newspaper late at night when only a skeleton crew was on duty. He would explain to whomever he found in charge that the wrong ad had inadvertently been supplied to the paper; he would then obligingly furnish a substitution. The new picture would show scantily clad females purportedly in the show. By the time someone noticed the switch, the new ad had already run, producing the desired sensation.[50] It was Alvord also who was credited by various sources with producing the Frontier Centennial's mocking slogan, "Fort Worth for entertainment; Dallas for education."[51]

The coup de grâce in Rose's advertising strategy was the sign. Erected by Rose's crews barely 500 feet outside the front gate of the central exhibition in Dallas, it brought the upstart Fort Worth festival within shooting distance of the gates of the fort. Towering 130 feet long and forty feet high, the sign portrayed a cowboy riding a bucking bronco and displayed prominently, in blinking neon letters over seventeen feet tall, the message, "Wild & Whoo-pee Forty-five Minutes West." Rose commissioned a local firm, the Corn Sign Company, to fabricate the sign and then leased space atop a Dallas building on the corner of First and Parry streets. Only a 250-foot Wrigley chewing gum sign in New York City was bigger. The Dallas Exposition Committee tried unsuccessfully in mid-May to rid themselves of the affront by persuading building inspectors to declare the building unsafe to support so large a structure and to rescind a previously granted construction permit. The scheme failed after Corn agreed to reduce the structure's height by twenty feet, and inspectors reinstated the permit. The sign with its teasing message beckoned to fairgoers with only minimal changes for the next two years. Meanwhile, committee members denied rumors that the central

exposition intended to erect its own competing sign outside the Fort Worth exposition.[52]

The sign brazenly announced Rose's intention to compete for centennial profits, aiming the neon message at outraged Dallas city fathers. They retaliated by issuing health cards to 2,400 prostitutes operating out of houses near the centennial grounds, loosening enforcement of gambling and liquor control laws, and opening the "Streets of Paris," an area of the midway devoted to the glorification of the more libidinal pleasures.[53] The same feature three years earlier at the 1933 Chicago Century of Progress Exposition had sparked controversy and lawsuits and had pulled in nearly a million paying customers. Some of the attractions

The neon sign advertising the Fort Worth Frontier Centennial. Erected just outside the main entrance of the Texas Centennial in Dallas, the sign (40 x 130 feet) proclaimed Billy Rose's intention to offer direct competition to the main exhibition.

Courtesy William E. Jary Photographic Collection, UTA.

included Mademoiselle Rou Pou, who disrobed behind a gauze curtain, leading one reporter to reason, "The gauze perhaps saved her from catching cold." Then there was Princess Poopadoop of the Street of All Nations, reaching out selflessly to the huddled masses with her banana dance. A reporter from the *Austin Statesman* noted, "She held the banana in somewhat the same fashion as Miss Liberty holds up her torch."[54]

For the price of admission at one popular concession, customers, after first being issued art pad and pencil, were marshalled into a crowded "Parisian artist's studio" to sketch undraped live models for a full minute and a half before being marshalled out again. *Fort Worth Press* columnist Jack Gordon tagged the models "ladies of easel virtue" and reckoned the new exhibit ". . . a good place to develop latent art talent. You sit down, gaze upon a completely nude model. . . . Lots of laughs in what the students draw." One customer was observed by an Austin reporter complaining to management because "not being particularly good with the crayons, he craved a Kodak."[55]

Not everyone viewed with favor the notoriety focused on the twin celebrations as a result of the competing "skin" campaigns. The *Houston Press* made light of the rivalry in an article impishly headlined, "The Battle of the Nudes." Still other writers openly criticized the tone and direction of the Fort Worth/Dallas competition, one complaining, "What with naked girls, cowboys and reproductions of frontier days in Texas . . . all history is forgotten, bitter commercialism is enthroned.[56] Local religious leaders also actively opposed Billy Rose's advertising strategies. A Methodist ministers' alliance framed a protesting resolution to present to the Fort Worth City Council, deploring "every influence that is being brought to bear to make our city appeal to [the] hoodlum element during the Centennial, rather than to a high-type American citizen. . . ."[57] When a committee of Baptist workers asked to see Rose to discuss reported "vulgarity" in show plans, he grew defensive and warned, "I will be glad to go over the complete plans of the show with any legitimate committee, but any pastor jumping on the show to get his name in the papers will get a cold reception." Eventually, Rose agreed to meet with the group, assuring its members that none of the centennial's major attractions would contain "girlie" shows. Later, however, he confided to reporters that while the group on the whole had seemed open minded, one of its members "looked as though he had sixty yards of rope under his hat waiting to hang you."[58]

The growing paranoia surrounding the controversy effectively concealed a hidden irony. As *Dallas* Morning *News* amusements editor John Rosenfield observed, "Ned Alvord's ads, posters and circulars have given off the impression of a saturnalia. 'March of Time' and the other propaganda stunts have exploited a sort of battle of sex display. The childish chauvinism will take an ironical turn on July 18. There isn't a naked woman on any of Billy Rose's stages. Only the peep shows house the nudity."[59] Rosenfield, a defender of the Frontier centennial even against other Dallas publications, publicly deplored the negative impact resulting from the undue focus on skin. He placed the blame at least partly on Ned Alvord's often-quoted slogan, "Fort Worth for entertainment; Dallas for education." He even dared to suggest that both cities had become unwitting pawns in Rose's career climb:

> No matter how Billy Rose has capitalized this sentiment in the Eastern papers, more to glorify his position on Broadway than to sell tickets in Fort Worth, it is essentially a boomerang. . . . it inspired the Dallas publicity department to bear down on its Midway attractions. If you ask us, Dallas has sold its Midway too hard. Its infinite variety and teetotal nudism have been hammered home. By picking up Mr. Rose's gauntlet, [Dallas] has all but ignored the educational and cultural features that make its fair great. We insist that the public interested in seeing an automobile made is four times greater than that interest [sic] in seeing how a woman is put together.[60]

CHAPTER 4

"ONLY A CRAZY NUT LIKE BILLY ROSE WOULD'VE DONE IT"

By late April an uncomfortable new reality began taking hold behind the scenes, one contrasting sharply with the rollicking face of preparations displayed for press and public. The shaky finances of the exposition had left it teetering on the edge of a fiscal precipice. James M. North presented figures to Amon Carter and the centennial board setting the estimated 1936 operating budget at $2,774,000, with a minimum of $911,000 required just to open. Of this pre-opening amount $750,000 was to be raised through bond sales, an additional $55,000 through concession rentals, and the remaining $106,000 coming through advance ticket sales.[1]

Several problems with the plan developed almost immediately. One of the most serious was the underestimation of materials and labor costs. Because of heavy overtime on the rushed project, by May 24 overruns of thirty-five to forty percent had pushed the $911,000 to $1,000,000. By June 10 an additional $100,000 was needed. This problem became further complicated by sluggish bond sales considerably below original estimates. Only $700,000 of the projected $750,000 had been raised. On June 15 James M. North wired Jesse H. Jones, director of Reconstruction Finance Corporation, "Frankly we have a bear by the tail and I am wiring you on my own initiative and without any consultation with others because of the knowledge you have steered so many others out of much larger difficulties. . . ." Five days later the crisis had become so acute that North reported, "We were unable to pay off our sub-contractors today and some of them are more or less frantic."[2]

While Carter and the bond committee tried to proselytize influential moneyed converts to the centennial cause, North became the forgotten pastor of the common pulpit, fighting desperately to secure day-to-day operating capital, requesting emergency loans from the WPA and Reconstruction Finance

Star-Telegram managing editor James M. North. North handled much of the day-to-day business and financing of the Frontier Centennial behind the scenes.

Courtesy Special Collections, UTA.

Corporation, an agency created in 1932 by Herbert Hoover to distribute $2 billion in emergency relief funds appropriated by Congress for industry and agriculture. In a letter to W. B. Costello requesting a loan of $175,000, North explained that bankers had already extended the centennial's credit line to the breaking point, taking $75,000 in profit bonds as collateral, underwriting their own loans for $75,000 more and agreeing to accept $25,000 of the original loan against the physical properties. He also revealed his personal anguish over the situation, saying, "After spending all my days and some sleepless nights trying to figure a way out of our difficulties, I can see none unless you come to our rescue with a loan. . . ." [3] On July 10, after additional persuasion from Amon Carter and Elliott Roosevelt, Jesse Jones agreed to loan the centennial $200,000, in addition to the $300,000 previously loaned to the organization by banks. Half the loan was to be secured by a mortgage on centennial property and the other half by a second $100,000 lien on all other physical assets.[4]

As the hundreds of personnel Billy Rose had assembled continued with frenzied round-the-clock preparations, spring gradually surrendered to the heat of the Texas summer. June 6, the day set for the official commencement of state centennial festivities, came and went. The Dallas Centennial Exposition and fairgrounds, despite some incomplete structures, opened on schedule to record crowds.

In Fort Worth, with show grounds still at least six weeks from completion and with millions of investment dollars in jeopardy, Rose made the decision to open the site to visiting reporters and columnists from across the country. *Time*, *Newsweek*, *Harper's*, *Literary Digest*, even *Country Gentleman* all sent representatives. Rose adopted the persona of dime-novel frontiersman for the benefit of arriving dignitaries and reporters. To achieve the right degree of western ambience for his office, by now shifted to one of the air-conditioned blockhouses at the centennial entrance, he decorated with cactus and a moose head and moved in a trio of penned wolves but kept Hungarian music going in the background.[5] He took to greeting newsmen from astride a white horse. After being made an honorary deputy by the sheriff, he also began sporting a cowboy outfit complete with gold badge and a gold-barreled revolver with a mother-of-pearl handle featuring a ruby-eyed gold steer's head. All this was worn, Rose claimed,

Billy Rose decked out in full western regalia for the benefit of visiting eastern reporters. *Time* magazine dubbed him "Billy the Kid."

Courtesy Special Collections, UTA.

"as protection against Dallas' angry city fathers." Lucius Beebe complained of the wolves "smelling to heaven" and declared Rose "the Broadway Barnum on horseback." After witnessing the goings on firsthand, Beebe characterized the preparations as "a Frontier Centennial of a six-gun order with overtones of Belshazzar's Feast, the Last Roundup and the McKinley Gold Parade. . . ." *Time* dubbed him "'Billy the Kid' Rose."[6] John Rosenfield, Jr., of the *Dallas News* noted, "Showmen and newspapermen who have been admitted to the grounds are unanimous in their praise of Rose's originality. . . ." but added ominously, "The only question is whether or not the big shows, with their $1 price, can do volume business and amortize."[7]

March of Time and *Metrotone* newsreel crews also arrived to film both the leggy chorines rehearsing production numbers for Casa Mañana and "Lady Godiva" riding nude through the Dallas Exposition's rival Streets of Paris show. The resulting ballyhoo prompted Colonel Andrew Jackson Houston, last surviving son of Texas hero and statesman General Sam Houston, to reflect dryly, "Is Texas celebrating its independence or the birth of musical comedy?"[8] A little later *Variety* slyly revealed that Lady Godiva was not nude after all but predicted smugly that no one would attend the Fort Worth show in an outdoor theater "because of the heat." On July 4 Ned Alvord's crews began distribution of a four-page special edition "newspaper," the "Frontier Centennial Longhorn," featuring pseudo accounts of Indian attacks, rustlers, and stagecoach robberies. Displayed prominently on the front page was the sketch of a bare-breasted cowgirl purporting to be Faye Cotton, "Texas Sweetheart Number One."[9] Inside, much enlarged reproductions of earlier advertising flyers, showing chorus girls splashing nude, now depicted the girls in modest swimsuits. Rose used the new ads to reiterate his claims that the main Dallas exposition "will be as pious and dull as a Canadian Sabbath." Dallas, he declared, "combines the smugness of Boston, the provincialism of Philadelphia; the snobbery of New York. . . ."[10]

Contradicting *Variety*'s dour pronouncement, the overall tone of the visiting press was awe at the massive preparations tempered with bewilderment over Rose's actions. *Newsweek* observed,

> Theatrical producers don't work during the Summer. They either jaunt to Europe to look over the foreign market or rummage around Hollywood and the cowbarn circuit for new plays and players. Billy Rose, who joined the big-league impresarios last Winter . . . is the individualist among them. The littlest showman of them all, he undertakes the biggest jobs and cares not a whit whether they are in season or out.[11]

Excitement ran through the collective copy: "Not since Santa Anna laid waste the Alamo and immortalized the names of Travis, Bowie and Davy Crockett has such a detonation rocked Texas," announced the *New York World Telegram*.[12] "Billy Rose and money plus John Murray Anderson," observed John Rosenfield of the *Dallas Morning News*, "could hardly avoid giving a good show.

Whether a good show in Fort Worth will hurt or help Dallas remains to be seen. But there is no power on earth to stop Fort Worth from producing a good show if it puts its mind to it. And the only sensible course for Dallas is to learn to live with this fact."[13] Rose's East Coast representative, Richard Maney, arrived prepared to do battle with his client, well aware of Rose's fondness for hyperbole. Instead, even he came away flabbergasted: "Mr. Rose is not above diving into the vat of exaggeration when inflamed with enthusiasm. But if the Frontier Centennial is not the most exciting and hilarious show that will erupt in our free states this summer, then I'll eat every adjective that I've ever typed."[14] Ernie Pyle, later to achieve fame in World War II as a daring and compassionate front-line correspondent, listened to the basic premise of the Casa Mañana Revue, "The Cavalcade of World Fairs," and explained to readers,

> A young couple go to the Chicago World's Fair on their honeymoon and then, getting the habit, they keep on going to fairs as the years roll by—to St. Louis, to San Francisco, and to Chicago's most recent Century of Progress . . . to the San Diego Fair and finally in the sunset of their days they wind up at the Fort Worth Frontier Centennial. And while this is going on, the gargantuan stage is reciprocating, revolving, swerving and probably oscillating a little, and then as a grand finale the whole stage moves floatingly backward on its limpid pool of real water and down into the lake . . . come real girls floating in real boats. That's the finale. What this has to do with the rest of the show I never find out.[15]

In the Pioneer Palace, Pyle explained, "they will have a bar something under two miles long, and everybody will be dressed as in the old days, and a 'tough' atmosphere will prevail. . . . there will be more six shooters than you'd find in the Colt Factory . . . . blood will flow like wine and the wine like water."[16]

Besides the approbation of the press, the Frontier Centennial and Casa Mañana had another factor in their favor—a solid lineup of talent. One of the biggest "name" stars set to appear was "King of Jazz" bandleader Paul Whiteman and his orchestra. Whiteman's popularity reached its zenith in the years between World War I and the Depression, a period that saw the decline of ragtime and the birth of the jazz age. His acclaim and rich orchestral style inspired numerous imitators and helped usher in the big band era. Whiteman, an old friend of Rose, had previously collaborated with him on *Jumbo*. For that show Rose asked Whiteman to make his entrance riding a white Arabian horse, leading his jazz band in marching uniforms. A portly, jovial man, Whiteman balked at the idea until Rose finally agreed to give him the horse if he went through with the stunt. He arrived in Fort Worth accompanied by the white horse and almost immediately became the city's unofficial ambassador of good will. Both he and his wife, actress Margaret Livingston, enthusiastically embraced the southwestern life style,

Bandleader Paul Whiteman is declared honorary mayor of Fort Worth.

Courtesy Special Collections, UTA.

purchasing horses, saddles, boots, and other gear. Whiteman leased the 400-acre Van Zandt farm outside Fort Worth where he rode for hours each day wearing an oversized western hat and black leather chaps personalized "Mr. P. W."[17]

Governor James Allred commissioned Whiteman as a colonel in the Texas Rangers, and on Paul Whiteman Day in Fort Worth, the musician became honorary mayor. He was photographed sitting behind the mayor's desk at city hall, sipping what became another of his trademarks—a glass of buttermilk. He became so fond of Texas buttermilk that he kept two pints ready each evening to drink between performances. Along with his band Whiteman brought several performers who had become well known through his weekly national radio program on NBC, including blues singer Ramona, Texas singer and dancer Durelle Alexander, and the hillbilly comedy trio, the Canovas. Throughout his stay, Whiteman continued his weekly national radio broadcasts from a popular Fort Worth nightspot, the Ringside Club, located at 1301 Jacksboro Highway.

Whiteman's fondness for Texas and Fort Worth was genuine. Long after the demise of Casa Mañana, he continued to express an interest in the city and returned often through the years for concert dates and to visit friends made during the centennial. Two local women, former Casa Mañana showgirls, encountered Whiteman several years later in New York City, where the two were performing at the CBS Theater in between the Casa Mañana summer seasons. In the brief conversation Whiteman expressed an interest in the progress of the girls' careers and learned that the two walked to and from the theater at night to save on expenses. For the rest of their stay in New York, a Whiteman band member appeared at the end of each evening's show to escort the girls home.[18]

Booked to fill Casa Mañana's second bandstand opposite Whiteman was Joe Venuti and his orchestra. The first great violinist of jazz, Venuti had first joined Paul Whiteman's band in 1929 but had to quit after being seriously injured in an auto accident. He rejoined the band in 1930.

To headline the impressive talent already lured to Fort Worth, Rose signed former Metropolitan Opera baritone Everett Marshall. Marshall made his Metropolitan debut at age twenty-five but eventually abandoned his operatic career for the more lucrative Broadway stage and movies. Marshall's deep, resonant baritone on such numbers as "Another Mile" and "The Night Is Young and You're So Beautiful" made him a favorite at Casa Mañana. Ann Pennington, star of both the Ziegfeld Follies and George White's Scandals for over a decade and good friend of Fanny Brice, was also featured in the revue. The tiny dancer, with a purported shoe size of only one-and-a-half, was to appear as "Little Egypt," the legendary belly dancer whose sensuous numbers scandalized America in 1904 at the St. Louis World's Fair. Other performers signed as feature acts included the dance team of Gomez and Winona, comedian Walter Dere Wahl, the Lime Trio, Gareth Joplin, and the Varsity Eight, although the official program listed this male octet as The Californians.

Ann Pennington and John Murray Anderson

Courtesy Special Collections, UTA.

Eddie Foy, Jr., replaced Jimmy Durante as the comic lead in the musical circus, *Jumbo*. Foy, his father and his six brothers and sisters—Charles, Richard, Irving, Bryan, Madeline, and Mary—had toured the old two-a-day vaudeville circuit as the Seven Little Foys, one of the most successful family acts ever to tread the boards. Seventy-five-year-old Josephine Demott Robinson, a performer with the old Barnum and Bailey Circus who billed herself as the oldest bareback equestrienne in entertainment, was in the musical's cast, and Edwin "Poodles"

Jumbo's Rosie the Elephant
Courtesy Special Collections, UTA.

Hanneford, one of the most beloved performers of Ringling Brothers and Barnum and Bailey Circus for many years, served as ringmaster.

Hanneford, who occasionally ventured into vaudeville in the off-season, gained fame with a "rough and tumble" act in which he would first pretend to lose his seat on the horse he was riding and then slide dangerously underneath the animal. Next, to the amazement of audiences he would climb back on the horse through its hind legs.[19] The Hanneford family could trace their origins as a performing troupe to the early 1800s. Over a century later the family was still touring, by now in its own show, the Hanneford Royal Canadian Circus. In 1915, to lure the troupe into signing with the Barnum and Bailey Circus, John Ringling agreed to purchase the entire Hanneford operation. Three generations of the Hanneford family performed in *Jumbo*: Hanneford's mother, Elizabeth, served as ringmistress; his wife, Grace, and his eighteen-year-old daughter, Grace Elizabeth, also appeared in the act. J. D. Ballard, the *Jumbo* giant, was a twenty-six-year-old native of Commerce, Texas. Towering above his fellow performers at 7'5", Ballard required specially made size fifteen shoes and size thirteen gloves.[20]

Rose conceived two brilliant ideas to pull attention away from the official exhibition in Dallas. One was the giant neon marquee advertising Fort Worth's Frontier Centennial, prominently located opposite the main entrance of the Dallas Centennial. The second was booking Sally Rand as the centerpiece attraction of Casa Mañana. Shrewd as well as beautiful, Rand had worked in nightclubs and appeared in movies for several years but first captured the national imagination during the 1933 Chicago Century of Progress Exposition where her dancing sparked fierce debate over accusations of obscenity and turned the dancer into an instant celebrity. The Chicago fair had confined its more salacious late-night enticements to an area of the midway called the "Streets of Paris," an attraction so unabashedly immodest that it pulled in a million tourists and led Dallas to appropriate the whole idea for the Texas Centennial. Rand was conspicuously absent from the Dallas "Streets."

Bathed in the deep blue spotlight that became her trademark and nude behind two large ostrich feather fans, the petite dancer performed to the strains of Beethoven's "Moonlight Sonata," Brahms' "Waltz in A-Flat," and other classical picks. She disdained the label "stripper" and permitted the audience to see only what she wished them to. "The Rand is quicker than the eye," she was fond of boasting. Her act, she maintained, was not a striptease but rather, a form of artistic expression which she preferred to style ballet divertissement.

In direct contrast to the notoriety of her public image, Sally Rand arrived at Fort Worth's Meacham Field aboard an American Airlines charter and immediately donned the prim, blue-and-white gingham dress handed her by Amon Carter. He loaded his prize trophy into a Conestoga wagon and escorted her back into town where she endeared herself to ladies' groups by scotching plans already publicized by Billy Rose to feature her number as a major sideshow lure. Hers, she

Sally Rand, featured attraction of the 1936 Casa Mañana Revue arrives in Fort Worth to begin rehearsals. Assisting her from the plane is producer Billy Rose.

Courtesy Special Collections, UTA.

asserted, was not that type of act, although she did agree, as a concession, to serve as hostess for the attraction, billed as the "Nude Ranch." The only ones publicly upset by Rand's arrival were Dallas "Streets of Paris" performers, including some with whom Rand had appeared at the 1933 Chicago exhibition. Mona Lleslie, the "Diving Venus" of the Dallas Centennial, complained to reporters that Rand's act was "as out of date as the bustle. She might be sophisticated, but she couldn't stand up to the gaff over here," evidently a reference to her own sideshow status as opposed to Rand's $1,000-dollar-a-week feature billing. Female barker Paris Peggy Hahn contributed to the sour grapes tone by adding, "Selling Sally Rand to the public would be just like trying to sell a 1907 car for modern transportation."[21]

Sally Rand was, in fact, a study in contrasts. Her first stop after arriving in Fort Worth was a breakfast in her honor at the downtown Fort Worth Club. There she chatted with invited dignitaries about politics and commerce and traded jelly recipes with wives who were not about to leave their husbands alone with her. *Press* reporter Jack Gordon, observing firsthand the strange dichotomy between her daring onstage persona and her private image, later recalled, "She was not only beautiful and sexy, but her knowledge was beyond belief. She was an intellectual. She could sit down and hold her own in any conversation—an amazingly brilliant woman."[22]

Throughout her stay in Fort Worth, she projected the same demure, ladylike image. She gave an afternoon tea for society club women in honor of her visiting mother and grandmother, then donned western garb again when she mounted a paint horse to direct—and stop—traffic in downtown Fort Worth. Photographers snapped her baking a cake in the kitchen of her rented apartment, piloting a locomotive, tossing out the ball that inaugurated Forest Park's first lighted baseball diamond, cutting the ribbon to open the newly refurbished Palace Theater, cuddling sheep, and even giving a pep talk to the Texas Christian University football squad.

Rand seemed genuinely bemused at the effect she had on people. At one point during the season's run, she injured her leg during the late performance of Casa Mañana and at the insistence of family members with whom she frequently traveled called a local hospital. She explained matter of factly to the physician on duty, "I'm Sally Rand, the fan dancer at Casa Mañana. I've been hurt and I want a doctor right away." The doctor, likely a young intern, had to ask her to repeat the request several times, but finally managed to stammer that perhaps she needed an older man. Still refusing to go to a hospital, Rand instead called Amon Carter, who put her in contact with his osteopathic physician, Dr. Phil Russell, whom Carter referred to as his "rubbin' doctor."[23]

All of Rand's activities were, in fact, carefully orchestrated to head off any protests. Indians of the Sioux nation, in Fort Worth to appear in "The Last Frontier," made her an honorary member of the tribe and christened her "White Fawn." In return, while *Metrotone News* filmed the event, she gave the tribe's dignified chief an impromptu lesson in fan dancing. She traveled to the state capital, Austin, where she was feted at various functions and explained to admirers, "My reputation has not been built on, shall we say, my being overdressed." Back in Fort Worth, she spoke to the Rotary Club, the Junior Chamber of Commerce, and the Advertising Club, telling its members, "I am an exponent of truth in advertising, and consequently I stick to the bare facts." Jack H. Hott, manager of the Chamber of Commerce, deadpanned, "We hope to see more of her."[24]

In June other out-of-town performers began arriving, led by a group of Indians who camped on their blankets outside Rose's office in the Sinclair Building until accommodations could be found for them.[25] Trains daily discharged an eclectic cargo of jugglers, acrobats, aerialists, trick riders, midgets, and musicians. Local reporters greeted all newcomers with fascinated interest, especially the train bearing twenty-eight dancers and showgirls from New York City. A special charter delivered the cast and menagerie of Billy Rose's *Jumbo*, an event coinciding ominously with the advent of the summer's first heat wave. Fanny Brice also made the scene, exciting rumors that Rose might feature her in Casa Mañana; she politely demurred, explaining that it would throw her into a higher tax bracket. Instead, while Billy worked, Fanny acted the part of the perfect housewife, busily passing the time in their hotel room stitching a dress for her friend Ann Pennington on a borrowed sewing machine.

The arrival of performers signaled the beginning of rehearsals for all major shows. Saloon girls from the "Pioneer Palace Revue" and sixty-eight teams of square dancers for "The Last Frontier" practiced can-can routines and clog steps under the incongruous direction of Alexander Oumansky, late of the Diaghileff Russian Ballet. Whooping cowboys perfected "shooting up" Sunset Trail in a dusty stampede of horses and men that ended in a break for refreshments at the Silver Dollar Saloon. Sheriff's deputies interrupted auditioning barkers to arrest one candidate on an Arizona felony warrant. Several *Jumbo* chorus members fainted from the heat, and Eddie Foy, Jr., threatened to quit if conditions did not improve. Over $300,000 had been spent to furnish the *Jumbo* building, first of the centennial structures to be completed with state-of-the-art sound, lighting, and

Casa Mañana under construction in the Spring of 1936.

Courtesy Special Collections, UTA.

stage equipment.[26] At the same time, the building had been designed virtually devoid of ventilation. Architects insisted that large double doors on opposite sides of the round building would admit sufficient crosscurrents for cooling when thrown open. Instead, the doors admitted only additional heat. The structure became a massive sauna where temperatures sometimes hit 112 degrees.[27]

Carpenters, electricians, and iron workers swarmed over Casa Mañana in around-the-clock shifts, racing to finish construction of the mammoth theater on schedule. Until the Casa stage was completed, choreographer Robert Alton and director John Murray Anderson ran showgirls and dancers through intricate production numbers at a blistering pace in the Monnig's Warehouse in downtown Fort Worth—a building without air-conditioning. Anderson demanded strict

Rehearsal of girls in the downtown Monnig's warehouse

Courtesy Special Collections, UTA.

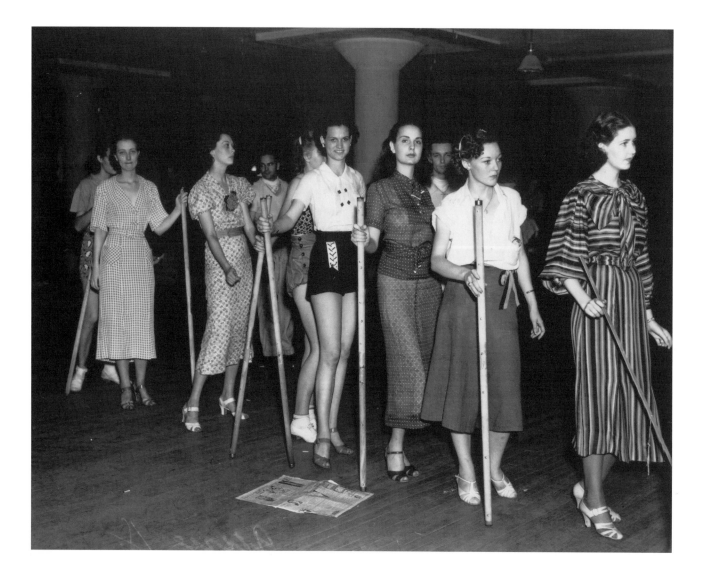

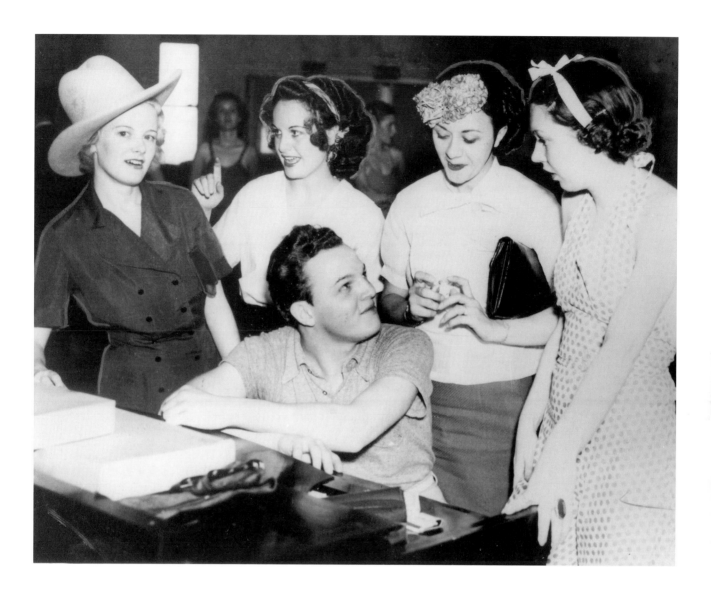

Lauretta Jefferson, right, popular assistant choreographer, with dancers in Monnig's Warehouse

Courtesy Special Collections, UTA.

obedience from his schoolgirl charges. Late arrival, talking, or wearing inappropriate jewelry resulted in fines that went into a kitty. The New York showgirls, though somewhat older and more sophisticated than their homegrown counterparts, were unfamiliar with southwestern decorum and visited businesses and diners in their rehearsal shorts to keep cool on lunch breaks. Protests from several local merchants prompted the posting of a sign in the rehearsal hall requesting girls to "dress decent" when going out.[28]

Some locals resented what they perceived as an attitude of elitism among Billy Rose's imported New York production team and showgirls. One staff member complained, "You get the feeling that we're big time stuff from Broadway, visiting down here for a few months to make a killing, and the sooner we get back to the big stem [New York] the happier we'll be."[29] This clash of East with West could sometimes lead to humorous confrontations. Scenic designer Albert Johnson stepped into a Main Street restaurant where he ordered coffee and buttered toast. The waitress, a no-nonsense type unfamiliar with New York dining customs, reappeared with the toast and a separate plate of butter. Johnson complained, "Say, I ordered buttered toast." Came the caustic reply, "Your arm ain't broke. Butter it yourself."[30]

As workers rushed to complete construction, Murray Anderson moved his charges to the Casa Mañana stage, where the sight of pretty chorus girls distracted carpenters and electricians but gave performers some welcome relief from the heat of their warehouse practice hall. Rehearsing amid enormous sets on the revolving stage proved challenging and sometimes even hazardous. As the stage began its turn at the conclusion of each scene, performers made a mad dash for specially provided quick-change rooms, where they sometimes had only one minute and forty-five seconds—the time it took the stage to complete one revolution—to change and race to their positions for the next scene. The precarious maneuver sidelined several dancers with twisted ankles and sprained knees. Coordinating the two orchestras led by Paul Whiteman and Joe Venuti also proved difficult. Situated at the two opposite extremes of the stage's 130-foot expanse, the two conductors could not see each other. Whiteman's solution to the nagging problem was not so much ingenious as practical. He attached a small light bulb to his baton and directed both bands from the island in front of the stage.[31]

Rehearsing near the picturesque lagoon could also be treacherous. Everett Marshall misstepped backstage during a late-evening session and plunged ungracefully into the water. As the stage crew helped him ashore, he vented his frustration on director Anderson, shouting, "Dammit, Murray, somebody's gonna have an accident and sue you for a million."[32]

One routine, the Triple Body Number, was specifically designed as a blackout, using only a strobe light for special effect. Teams of chorus members donned awkward, black velvet costumes on which skeletons had been painted. Olive Nicolson, one of the ensemble dancers remembered, "One girl would be all black with just the left leg and rib cage; [another] girl had the right leg. They would get together so it looked like the bones dancing." The third member of each team functioned as the skeleton's head. The number worked beautifully during early rehearsals, but in final rehearsals, under blackout conditions, dancers became disoriented. Nicolson recalled: "One girl would fall in the water [because] you couldn't tell where you were going. [Team members] would all be trying to find their bodies . . . because it was so confusing." After several mishaps under night-time conditions, Anderson and Rose scrapped the routine.[33]

Problems of a different nature surfaced during rehearsals of "The Last Frontier." The Wild West show featured among its attractions an artificial mountain, a herd of buffalo, several different New Mexico and Arizona Indian

Interior of Casa Mañana with revolving stage slid back to reveal the moat and water curtain. Workmen rush to complete repairs and adjustments.

Courtesy Special Collections, UTA.

tribes in mock battle, a wagontrain, trick riding and marksmanship demonstrations, and finally, what was billed as the "world's largest square dance." Among these acts Rose interspersed what he described as "Wild West Rodeo Events, timed and staged to keep you sitting on the edge of your seat." Wranglers nightly maneuvered the cantankerous bison herd into position by means of a concealed tunnel running through the artificial mountain. The 2,000-pound beasts could not be trusted to mind their cues. During an evening rehearsal, one buffalo, evidently anxious for feature billing, broke from the herd and stampeded over the manmade hill. Rose, unaware that the renegade had departed from the script, had to be hauled to safety atop a nearby fence, where he gasped to Murray Anderson, "Let's don't do that anymore. Have them all come down the regular trail."[34] After several such mishaps, Verne Elliott, longtime rodeo producer for the Fort Worth Stock Show, quipped, "Better call it 'The Lost Frontier,' Billy."[35]

Rose, the upstart, abrupt Jewish boy from Hell's Kitchen, frequently suffered culture shock trying to comprehend western ways. Cowboys, especially the taciturn Elliott, unsettled him. Reporter Mary Wynn remembered, "Elliot was the only person that could intimidate Billy Rose, just one of these real tough guys [who] didn't say much, but he could really eye you down. He needed to be tough handling all the cowboys and stock. He was a real cowboy. He wasn't going to take anything off [Rose]."[36] Rose chain-smoked incessantly but never seemed to have any cigarettes despite a compulsion for keeping his pockets stuffed full of cash. One day during a rehearsal of "The Last Frontier" Rose found himself standing alongside a trio of drovers and, simultaneously, in need of a cigarette. He barked his demand for a smoke to no one in particular but got no response. After he repeated the request a second time, one of the cowboys, with a calculated, sidelong glance at his companions, took the well-chewed, hand rolled butt out of his own mouth, passed it to Rose, and waited for a reaction. Rose hesitated momentarily, staring, then took the offering and shoved it in his own mouth. The rehearsal went on. Mary Wynn was standing close by watching the confrontation. "He [Rose] didn't dare turn it down, because for two cents they might have just lifted him up and thrown him over the fence."[37]

A problem of a more delicate nature developed in another scene during which Indian braves made a dramatic, single file entrance along the crest of the artificial mountain. Rose had imported members of several different tribes, including Comanche, Sioux, and Navajo. Each time the mixed group rehearsed the episode several tribesmen entered bunched closely together, spoiling the effect. Finally, Rose ordered a halt, hoping to discover the problem. Word came back that since three of the men were chiefs, these three must all lead. Unfazed by a total ignorance of tribal politics, Rose barked to production assistants, "Make 'em all chiefs!" His stumbling attempt at cultural sensitivity seemed to mollify the gentlemen. For the remainder of the centennial, the Indians made the entrance as Rose wished—in single file.[38]

With the grand opening of the Frontier Centennial set for July 18, Rose accelerated the already-frenetic pace of preparations in late June, ordering all-night work crews for the many remaining incomplete structures and adding all-night rehearsals for major shows. On June 28, in a carefully timed public relations move, he threw open the centennial gates to admit locals for a preview. Five thousand of the curious showed up, braving afternoon temperatures in the upper nineties for a chance to gawk at the exhibition's major pavilions. During the first week of July, Texas' capricious weather threatened to jeopardize this delicate timetable. Thunderstorms accompanied by high winds smashed through the show grounds, seriously damaging the partially completed sets in Casa Mañana. The city council was forced to vote emergency funds for repairs so that workmen could construct thirty-foot windbreaks to head off further problems.

Vagaries of climate, financing, and human nature seemed only to intensify interest in Casa Mañana's unveiling in the days before the premiere. Society columnists painstakingly recorded preparations for the opening gala, supplying details of parties and lists of first-nighters table by table. Like a nervous parent anxious for unruly children to make a good impression, the *Star-Telegram* reported,

> Reservations for the Casa Mañana opening have been made for weeks.
> Women have searched for their most ravishing gowns to wear and their
> handsomest jewels, for society will be on parade; the eyes of the United

States will be on the opening of the Frontier Centennial, of which Casa Mañana will be an unparalleled event. [39]

One society maven complained peevishly that no special entrance had been provided for elaborately attired first-nighters.

One day before the official opening, on Friday, July 17, Billy Rose and Amon Carter jointly hosted a second preview of the Casa Mañana Revue for over 1,000 magazine, radio, and newspaper editors and writers from across the United States. The press blitz had been carefully orchestrated by Billy's New York press agent, Richard Maney, whose job was to make sure the liquor flowed liberally before and after the show. The guest list ranged from some of the largest and most influential dailies in the country to such obscure papers as the *Forney Messenger*, the *Gilmer Daily Mirror*, the *Hockley County Herald*, the *Leon County News*, the *Farmersville Times* and the *Pittsburg* (Texas) *Gazette*. The guest list of prominent writers, which read like a veritable Who's Who of Journalism, included Robert Garland of the *New York World Telegram*, Whitney Bolton of *Literary Digest*, John Lardner of the North American Newspaper Alliance, Damon Runyon of King Features, and Burns Mantle of the *New York Daily News*. After the invited guests had dined, Amon Carter stepped up to the rostrum to deliver the official welcome and to reiterate claims made in an earlier radio broadcast that "There was no thought of competition with the Texas Centennial Exposition in Dallas." Calling it the outstanding world's fair to date in the United States, Carter asserted, "We are 100 per-cent behind the Dallas exposition, and we want Dallas to come to ours. It might do you city folks some good to visit the country folks once in a while." Carter next introduced Billy Rose as "the most ingenious and hard working little cuss and the greatest guy I know of." Rose, tie-less and looking haggard from lack of sleep, responded to the approbation, adding, "As far as I am concerned, Amon Carter is the Fort Worth Frontier Centennial." The show, billed as a dress rehearsal, ran smoothly, leading John Rosenfield to suspect that the few stops were "obviously a cunning demonstration of methods for the benefit of the newspapermen."[40]

Billy Rose's Texas-size gamble had paid off. At the conclusion of the final scene, the invitation-only audience leaped spontaneously to its feet to give Rose,

Anderson, and Carter a rowdy standing ovation. The critics vied with each other to find superlatives worthy of the show. Robert Garland called the Revue "a stage show glorified out of all knowing. I can't tell you the half of it. Casa Mañana is as big as Texas." Richard Maney added, "For valor, valor touched with profligacy, I give you Fort Worth, even if it suspects all scotch drinkers of being sissies."[41] Even the usually reserved *New York Times* seemed at a loss for words:

> "Plenty," in the argot of our avenues, is the verdict of eyewitnesses returned from the scene of the commotion. Gentlemen famed for their veracity raise their hands high and solemnly state that in the Casa Mañana Mr. Rose presents a spectacle that has no parallel in our curdled world . . . Set it up in Central Park, says its applauders . . . and it would run through more Summers than "Abie's Irish Rose."[42]

Rose's own advertising master, Deacon Ned Alvord, reportedly sagged in his chair at the Revue's conclusion moaning, "I'm ruined! It's even better than I said it was!" [43]

The commentary of rival Dallas pundits was equally unrestrained in praise of the show. Calling the show, "staggering," *Morning News* columnist John Rosenfield proclaimed, "The show beggars description. . . . Two hundred girls and principals and sets larger than life fill the 130-foot stage." He termed the Revue, "Billy Rose's valid bid for international attention," and conceded, "We doubt that anything else so large or sumptuous has risen from the pavements of the world's capitals let alone the Texas prairie."[44] Jimmy Lovell, theater critic of the rival *Times-Herald*, agreed:

> Billy Rose has taken what apparently has been a bottomless hole and has produced a show which undoubtedly will cause Broadway to lift its eyes into the air and wonder whether Texas is a state or a gold mine. . . . the management has produced a series of spectacles which challenge the use of all the "rave" synonyms in the dictionary. . . . it is one of the most fabulous affairs which could be offered by the most imaginative showman.[45]

Fairfax Nisbet of the evening *Dallas Journal* paraphrased Julius Caesar to add, ". . . we went to Fort Worth, we saw, and will break down and confess we were conquered . . ."[46] *Fort Worth Press* columnist Jack Gordon rhapsodized,

Never before have there been so many girls on a single stage. Never before was there a stage large enough to accommodate them. Never before have such huge stage sets been built. Not once before were so many lights trained on one stage. Here is something to make Ziegfeld turn in his grave—in sheer admiration.[47]

Paul Whiteman reduced the entire matter to eleven words: "Only a crazy nut like Billy Rose would have done it."[48]

THE COWBOYS, THE INDIANS, AND SALLY RAND

By opening day, July 18, both performances of the Casa Mañana Revue had sold out. At 3:00 P.M. a Wells Fargo stagecoach bearing Governor James Allred, Senator Tom Connally, American Airlines President C. R. Smith, Amon Carter, and other dignitaries left the Texas & Pacific Railway Station for the centennial show grounds. Carter, sporting western garb and armed with a revolver, rode next to Verne Elliott, who handled the team. Seated behind them, Elliott Roosevelt rode shotgun, guarding the money box. At precisely 3:30 P.M., President Franklin Roosevelt, a longtime friend of Carter, interrupted his Maine fishing trip long enough to press a button onboard the presidential yacht, *Sewanna*. By means of an elaborate transcontinental hookup, the button activated a radio impulse which traveled first by wireless to the USS *Potomac*, then to a Maine relay station where it was transmitted via telegraph 3,000 miles to Texas. At the main entrance of the Sunset Trail, the tiny impulse triggered a knife, which then severed a ribbon attached to a cowboy lariat, officially opening the Fort Worth Frontier Centennial. Simultaneously Mrs. Verne Elliott and another unnamed club woman shattered bottles of expensive champagne across a couple of entrance turnstiles. Four months and eight days had passed since the original groundbreaking ceremony.[1]

On opening day 25,000 customers poured through the centennial's main gates, paying prices that ranged from 50 cents for a general admission ticket, to $1 for the celebration's major attractions, *Jumbo* and Casa Mañana.[2] At the centennial entrance, built to resemble a stockade complete with twin blockhouses,

Frontier Centennial opening day, July 18, 1936. A Wells Fargo coach transports Amon Carter (2ⁿᵈ from left), Elliott Roosevelt (3ʳᵈ from left), and other dignitaries to the centennial grounds.

Courtesy Special Collections, UTA.

visitors passed under large letters angled crazily overhead proclaiming, "Wher The Wezt Begins" [sic]. The stagecoach full of dignitaries proceeded up Sunset Trail to the Last Frontier pavilion, where it was "held up" by daring masked bandits. The *Star-Telegram* reported tongue-in-cheek, "Guns barked as stagecoach passengers resisted vainly. They finally were forced to alight with hands aloft. At this critical juncture, the United States Cavalry rescued, dispersing the bandits with volleys of gunfire."[3]

Dedicatory speeches ensued, a congratulatory telegram from the president was read, and the entire scene was repeated so that *Movietone* newsreel crews could record the event for posterity.[4] The premiere of the first show, "The Last

Frontier," surpassed Rose's earlier prediction of "keeping the audience on the edge of their seats." Narrator Captain Irving O'Hay intoned, "Many moons ago, the smile of the Great Spirit beamed upon the land of the Red Man. Great herds of shaggy buffalo thundered westward." A short time later Chuck Williams, the cowboy around whose adventures the plot loosely revolved, made his entrance in a bronc-busting episode on a horse appropriately named "Sundown." In an unchoreographed maneuver, horse and rider cartwheeled spectacularly into the pool at the base of the mountain's artificial waterfall. Not until several moments later—and much to the relief of the audience—did Williams crawl from the water, soaked but unhurt. Sundown, less sure of his role in the proceedings, had

Dana Suesse, composer of many of the songs for the 1936 and 1937 Casa Mañana Revues, including "The Night Is Young and You're So Beautiful." A child prodigy, she had her Carnegie Hall debut as a teenager.

Courtesy Special Collections, UTA.

to be roped and ungracefully towed to the edge of the pool before the show could continue. Behind the scenes, there was confusion also. Thirty cantankerous buffalo had their parts cut from the script, and an Indian war party missed its cue to attack. The warriors were finally tracked down behind the artificial mountain where they were taking part in a live broadcast over a national network.[5]

At precisely 6:30 P.M., Casa Mañana swung wide its gates to receive first-nighters. The heat did little to wilt the high spirits of merrymakers who danced to the rhythms of Joe Venuti's orchestra on the wide expanse of the revolving stage and dined on a menu that offered fare ranging from 40-cent hamburgers and 30-cent beer to prime rib for $1.50. A complete dinner, consisting of tomato juice or soup du jour, sirloin steak garnished with bordelaise sauce, baked Idaho potato, salad, string beans, bread, and choice of beverage went for $2.00, a bargain even in that day. The state's tough liquor laws remained theoretically in effect, but the Liquor Control Board, in a move designed to increase centennial revenues and promote out-of-state tourism, agreed to ignore liquor consumption and sales. Casa Mañana offered a wide selection of imported and domestic wines, with a ten-year-old bottle of Piper Heidsieck champagne going for the top price of $7.50. Wine by the glass could be had for as little as 35 cents.[6] By contrast, the Dallas Centennial Exposition served no alcoholic refreshments of any kind, except for what could be purchased from a package store located on the centennial grounds.[7]

As the sunset faded behind Casa Mañana's archways, Paul Whiteman stepped to his position at center stage and raised his lighted baton. At his signal, the two bands swung into the opening fanfare, and the voice of announcer Tommy Gleason boomed out, "Billy Rose presents—the Casa Mañana Revue!" Simultaneously, Carlton Winckler's battery of spotlights, the strongest ever assembled to that time, sprang to life, and the center of the mammoth stage began to glide back dramatically, revealing the water-filled lagoon. Then slowly, the million-pound structure began to revolve, unveiling scenic designer Albert Johnson's fanciful interpretation of the 1904 St. Louis World's Fair, featuring a Viennese sidewalk cafe and three towering orange-and-white minarets whose onion domes twinkled with scores of sparkling lights. Showgirls and boys dressed

St. Louis World's Fair Scene, Casa Mañana 1936.

Courtesy Fort Worth Public Library.

as St. Louis belles and beaus strolled about the scene. A girl in bloomers and a boy in peg-leg trousers pedaled across the stage on a bicycle built for two as The Californians serenaded the audience with such turn-of-the-century favorites as "Meet Me In St. Louis," "The Good Old Summertime," "Oh, You Beautiful Doll," "Daisy, Daisy," and "Why Do They Call Me a Gibson Girl?" Featured prominently in the musical numbers were what one writer described as the "breathtaking lovelies" of Billy Rose's hand-picked chorus line "who enacted at a dizzying pace a dozen romantic, sentimental episodes of the period."[8]

Next came Ann Pennington in her daring imitation of Little Egypt, her entrance heralded by, "Watch her shake, not a bone in her body, like a bean in a bowl of jelly." Finally, as baritone Everett Marshall crooned, "The Night Is

Star-Telegram publisher Amon G. Carter at his memento-filled desk. Photographs of Will Rogers and Casa Mañana are prominently displayed.

Courtesy Special Collections, UTA.

Young and You're So Beautiful," Faye Cotton entered, draped in a $5,000 gold mesh gown to begin her reign as "Texas' Sweetheart Number One." Executed by New York jewelers Whiting and Davis, the gown boasted a fifteen-foot train weighing between forty and fifty pounds.[9]

The stage revolved again to reveal the Paris Exposition of 1925, a set characterized by one reporter as "gay and sprightly with spangled purples."[10] Five thousand miniature light bulbs outlined the Eiffel Tower and twin revolving Ferris wheels. Showgirls in ornate costumes and spangled headdresses paraded against the backdrop of a Parisian sidewalk cafe and park, representing such legendary Parisian locales as Maxim's, Casino de Paris, the Latin Quarter, the

Opera, the Moulin Rouge, and Folies Bergère. High-kicking dancers executed a rousing can-can followed by comic tumblers The Lime Trio, and Gomez and Winona, an adagio dance team who "raise ballroom stepping to the dignity of genuine ballet."[11]

As the stage made its circuit revealing one gorgeous set after another, applause repeatedly drowned out the music. But it was the third scene, built around the 1933 Chicago Century of Progress Exposition, that elicited the most enthusiastic response from the audience. The thinly veiled undercurrent of anticipation became almost palpable as the lights deepened to blue, and Sally Rand, a vision of graceful, luminous sensuality, stepped from a niche within the

1936 Texas Sweetheart Number One, Faye Cotton, models the $5,000 "gold" mesh gown created by New York jewelers Whiting and Davis.

Courtesy Special Collections, UTA.

Chorus members and showgirls rehearse Parisian scene from 1936 "Cavalcade of World's Fairs." Costumes of showgirls represented well-known Parisian locales.

Courtesy Special Collections, UTA.

curves of a modernistic wall to perform her ballet divertissement. Billy Rose had pronounced her fan routine "dated," so Rand performed the dance with a huge opaline balloon designed to specifications by the Goodyear Rubber Company. Her accoutrements made little difference—the Rand presence held the audience spellbound. Even *Star-Telegram* music critic E. Clyde Whitlock, whose usual copy ran to symphony concerts and chamber music recitals, succumbed to the Rand mystique: "The petite figure of the dancer toys with an enormous bubble with charming grace and illusion. The music is hot and jazzy, but never cheap, and the furiously fast clicking feet of the hordes of dancing girls is exhilarating."[12]

The final scene opened with Everett Marshall's stirring rendition of "Another Mile." Listed vaguely as a "Masque of Texas," the episode contained little recognizable history but paraded several dozen showgirls and dancers past the audience in scanty gold costumes reputed to symbolize Texas under the six flags of France, Spain, Mexico, the Republic, the Confederacy, and the United States. There were even "Indians" wearing flashy, gold-feathered headdresses. Everett Marshall sang "Lone Star," Venetian gondolas floated incongruously across the lagoon, and Ann Pennington popped out of a papier-mâché "hundred gallon" cowboy hat. As the evening's grande finale, sixty-four jets of water lit by

Everett Marshall performing in 1936.

Courtesy Special Collections, UTA.

Grand finale of 1936 Casa Mañana Revue, "A Masque of Texas." Dancers paraded in scanty gold "cowgirl" costumes and Ann Pennington popped out of a papier-mâchè "hundred gallon" cowboy hat.

Courtesy Special Collections, UTA.

dozens of rainbow-colored lights suddenly erupted from the lagoon, and the combined orchestras of Whiteman and Venuti broke into "The Eyes of Texas," bringing the audience jubilantly to its feet singing, whistling, and cheering. This outpouring of enthusiasm from the crowd proved more startling to representatives of the *New York Times* sent to cover the premiere than the show's visual excesses. They reported,

> Texans are not given to polite applause. Pleased with what is revealed to their eye and ear they stand and give vent to variations of the rebel yell, hands cupped over mouth in the fashion of harmonica players. Only when bored does their recognition sink to the level of hand clapping.[13]

By the third or fourth day of the centennial, as the initial glow of the premiere faded, problems began to develop, many related directly to the heat. On opening day, July 18, the mercury reached ninety-nine, and for the next several days the heat wave stretched on unabated. *Jumbo*, already in trouble because of its poorly ventilated building, suffered the worst. Despite the addition of several large water-cooled fans, the show had to be pared from its original running time of two hours to one. The sound system also failed, necessitating elimination of much of the show's libretto. Eddie Foy, Jr., who had endured three weeks of rehearsing under less-than-ideal conditions, had his entire part cut—after only six performances. A python in one of the sideshows expired—reportedly from heatstroke. By July 22, only four days into the run, the centennial board scaled back the exposition from its original 11:00 A.M. opening to 5:00 P.M. when the atmosphere was cooler. The heat did little, though, to discourage the sweating thousands that continued to pour into the centennial. Mule drawn, blue-and-white miniature prairie schooners and rickshaws fashioned to resemble covered wagons ferried visitors around the grounds, the latter pulled by college students

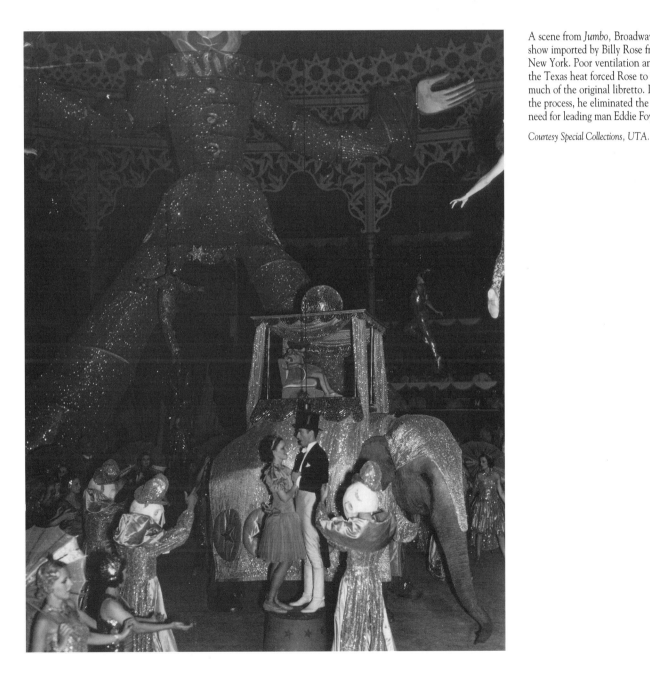

A scene from *Jumbo*, Broadway show imported by Billy Rose from New York. Poor ventilation and the Texas heat forced Rose to trim much of the original libretto. In the process, he eliminated the need for leading man Eddie Foy, Jr.

Courtesy Special Collections, UTA.

from various Texas universities. In the evenings, the same conveyances remained available to cart inebriated guests to the front gate after Casa Mañana's final show.[14]

At the Pioneer Palace, the steamy interior assumed the raucous character of a boom-town honky-tonk where revelers danced, tried their luck at the nickel slot machines, or pressed against the bar six deep to hear Lulu Bates, dressed in a red-sequined gown, sing, "I'm In Love With a Handlebar Moustache" to Tom Patricola. Song sheets placed on tables encouraged customers to join in, with the admonition, "If you can't sing good, sing loud."[15] Equally popular were the Six Tiny Rosebuds—Florence Mann, Mildred Monti, Betty Pryor, Nella Plaston,

Pioneer Palace Band & Lulu Bates.
Courtesy Special Collections, UTA.

Muriel Fuller, and Helen Summers—an oddly matched team of lady dancers. The smallest Rosebud weighed in at 215 pounds; the largest at 340. The "Honky Tonk Parade" recreated the "Small Time Revue," the concept Billy Rose had first introduced in his Casino de Paree and Music Hall. The lyrics from the original revue alluded to the dream of every unknown vaudevillian who never "played the Palace" and set the stage for the eclectic offering of talent that appeared each evening:

> "Within a thousand barrooms
> We have made them laugh and cry,
> But *Variety* won't notice us,
> Until the day we die."[16]

Besides the Rosebuds, the Honky Tonk Parade cast included torch singer Lily Chambers; Eddie Eddy, the man with crying glasses; bell ringer Billy Hess; Hy Town, a breakdown comedian; Rène and June Melva, musical bottle instrumentalists; Clowntino, comic mandolin musician; and spoon artist Jack Spoons. E. Clyde Whitlock, who in addition to his duties as music critic, served as head of the violin department of the Fort Worth Conservatory, dutifully covered every aspect of the Frontier Centennial, including his evaluation of the "Honky Tonk Parade": "The Pioneer Palace provides a lusty program of down-by-the-tracks music, cabaret style, for those who like that sort of thing. It sounds fast and loud, which are the requisites for the type."[17] In contrast to earlier New York outings, where the cross section of eccentric acts "represented the despair born of the futility of the inept," the *New York Times* reporter noted approvingly the favorable reception given the small-timers by centennial crowds. In the Pioneer Palace, he observed, "[Texans] accept the performers—fire-eaters, bellringers, clubswingers—as topnotchers rather than professional defaulters."[18]

As the centennial's premiere date approached, Billy Rose had openly admitted to the existence of several "peep" shows, capitalizing freely on the publicity generated by the controversial nature of such attractions. One, billed as "Beauty and the Beast," featured "La Femme Nue," bare-breasted Laurene NeVell, who danced in a cage containing several lions. The presence of the big cats no doubt served as a potent deterrent for the more rowdy customers who felt the urge to take a closer look. Later in the season, NeVell was replaced with the "Ziegfeld Milk Bath," starring a blonde who twenty-five times a day stepped out of her clothes and into a glass tub containing water and powdered milk. But by far the most popular and controversial of the sideshow attractions was Sally Rand's Nude Ranch, billed euphemistically as an "educational exhibit."[19] Rand's duties between shows in Casa Mañana included serving as hostess and greeter. The building housing the Ranch was an attraction in itself, featuring what one newspaper described as towering, undraped "Venus-like" female figures on either side of the entrance. Flaming red hair crowned each goddess, her raised arms appearing to support the roof in a garish imitation of a Grecian caryatid. Two voluptuous figures perching atop the roof reclined provocatively against the words, "*Dude Ranch*," the "D" crossed out and replaced with "N" to become "*Nude Ranch*."

Sally Rand's Nude Ranch, 1936. Reclining nudes on roof have been discreetly removed by photographer.

Courtesy Dalton Hoffman private collection.

Sally and Her Nude Ranch 'Hands' Gather at Drift Fence at the Fort Worth Frontier Centennial in 1936.

Courtesy Special Collections, UTA.

Inside the ranch fifteen girls, all of them bare-breasted except for oversized green bandanas, lounged "with nothing to prevent them from benefiting from the Texas night air." They sat on horseback, tossed beach balls, pitched horse-shoes and shot arrows at targets. Lending further eccentricity to the scene, each girl sported a ten-gallon cowboy hat, western boots, and a pair of holstered six-shooters. Nude Ranch personnel "rehearsed" by taking archery instruction from a local expert and lariat-twirling lessons from several local firemen who did not require much encouragement to volunteer for the extra duty. As an afterthought almost, an obvious temptation occurred to someone, and a floor-to-ceiling wire screen was installed to separate the patrons from the girls. Customers paid 50 cents to enter and were required to check cameras at the entrance. One satisfied patron, a weathered rancher at least seventy-five years old found another way around the restrictions. He entered the Nude Ranch at 3:30 P.M. and remained until 8:00 P.M.—all on one ticket.[20]

Helping preside over the Nude Ranch was its only male, Adolph, self-described "King of the Nudists." Adolph, who claimed to be seventy-five, habitually sported sandals and khaki shorts characterized by *Press* amusements columnist Jack Gordon as "air-conditioned panties."[21] From the Nude Ranch the 'king' gave health lectures on the values of exercise and eating natural foods. Adolph himself claimed such devotion to his philosophy that he could not bear staying shut up indoors and habitually slept in convenient haystacks and pastures. Soon after his arrival in Fort Worth, Adolph experienced a sudden philosophical spasm after encountering a violent West Texas thunderstorm. A short while later, he was observed checking quietly into the downtown Texas Hotel for a healthful night's sleep—indoors.[22]

The publicity campaign leading up to the grand opening had intensified the controversy over the appearance of Sally Rand and the promotion of the peep shows in the dueling centennial exhibitions. Some small-town weeklies covered "The Last Frontier" and *Jumbo*, more family-oriented shows, but pointedly ignored Sally Rand and Casa Mañana, perhaps fearing the reproaches of conservative subscribers. Still others, like the editor of the *Palestine Daily Herald* made allusion to the controversy while still offering cautious praise: "Somehow people have come to expect big shows to be naughty, and the bigger the naughtier. . . . It [Casa Mañana] was something of an innovation . . . unexpected, but gratifying . . . "[23] Italy, a small community southeast of Fort Worth sent two representatives, who seemed relieved at having survived the experience:

> K. G. Stroud and George Couch were in Fort Worth last Friday night and attended a preview of the Frontier Centennial. They brought back a very favorable report of the show and said it was all anyone could expect in the way of entertainment. They did not appear to be unduly excited over Sally Rand and her performances.[24]

Some larger dailies, like the *Austin Statesman*, continued to complain openly about the proliferation of nude and suggestive shows, characterizing attempts

to quell such acts as "half hearted" and "posed for an expected flop." Citing
a lackadaisical attitude on the part of centennial board members and other state
officials, the newspaper observed that the state attorney general's office had
refused to rule on the public decency of such shows based on the rather flimsy
excuse that none of the local centennial boards had requested such a legal
opinion. Both state and local officials seemed eager, in fact, to avoid any confrontation on the issue altogether despite the existence of a board of censors
appointed by the forty-third legislature as part of the centennial appropriation
act.[25] The implication seemed clear—if no one was objecting, no action was
required. Meanwhile, spielers of the infamous "Streets of Paris" in Dallas concessions continued to guarantee that if the subjects of all the peeking did not take
off everything, patrons' money would be refunded.

Despite the ongoing controversy or perhaps because of it, as the summer
advanced, Fort Worth became a magnet for high rollers, senators, congressmen,
and show business luminaries. The attention heartened centennial officials, but
James North and banker John Sparks insisted on continuing what had become a
nightly ritual—counting cars in the centennial parking lot.[26] Amon Carter took
advantage of the favorable critical comments generated by the grand opening of
Casa Mañana to push for $100,000 in unallocated funds from the U.S.
Centennial Commission. Calling the centennial's ongoing financial crisis
"acute," in telegrams to Vice President John Nance Garner, Secretary of
Agriculture Henry A. Wallace, and Secretary of State Cordell Hull, he pleaded
that the Frontier Centennial was providing jobs for 3,300 previously out-of-work
citizens. Within days he had his answer—no more loans.[27] At the downtown
Blackstone Hotel few, if anyone, took note of the crisis going on behind the
scenes. Bellhops continued to pocket as much as $100 a day in tips.[28] On the
centennial grounds, box seats, a private bar, and luxurious lounge rooms on the
theater's plush second level continued to cater to the specialized whims of the
VIP crowd. Admission to the exclusive enclave, by invitation only, required a
$50 enrollment fee, with membership limited to 250 of Fort Worth's upper crust
and their guests. Rose hired legendary race car driver Barney Oldfield to serve as
greeter for the celebrity crowd and official host of the exhibition.

Novelist Ernest Hemingway, on his way across the country with his family, spied Ned Alvord's posters and took a long detour through Fort Worth, just to satisfy his curiosity.[29] Talent scouts haunted the grounds, and movie directors, including Howard Hawks, took in the Casa Mañana Revue. Local newspapers reported offers of screen tests to several of the more attractive dancers and showgirls. Film entrepreneur Aubrey Kennedy toured the centennial grounds and discussed with Rose the possibilities of leasing "The Last Frontier" set to film a western movie featuring cowboy star Hoot Gibson. The deal never materialized.[30]

MGM sent four truckloads of equipment and a crew to film a two-reel short of the Casa Mañana Revue. Billy Rose was among those appearing in the film but declined to accept a fee for his work. After Rose viewed his screen debut, an MGM executive asked him for a self-appraisal of his efforts: "You don't see actors who look like me working on my stage do you?" he quipped. The completed film went out to theaters with an accompanying booklet, offering publicity suggestions:

> For a stunt that cannot fail to bring you a spread of pictures in your newspapers, announce that all local "shorties," "shrimps," and "half-pints" are to be admitted free as guests of the theater and their diminutive host, Billy Rose. To make this more interesting you might place a bar across one entrance door under which the undersized would have to pass to qualify for admittance.[31]

Vice President and Mrs. Garner, Army Air Corps flying ace Major Jimmy Doolittle, FBI Director J. Edgar Hoover, Broadway producers Earl Carroll and George White, and former heavyweight boxing champ Max Baer all added their names to the list of notables visiting Fort Worth. One southern governor, while in town for the festivities, requested an escort backstage so that he could speak with his old friend, dancer Sally Rand. Billy Rose himself ushered the governor to her dressing room, where Rand invited both in. The two men entered to discover Rand lounging on the floor reading the Bible—in the nude. The unperturbed governor accepted a proffered chair, and he and Rand began discussing the passage she had been studying.[32]

Screen star Ginger Rogers, a local success, angered hometown admirers when she appeared at the Dallas Centennial for two performances but apparently snubbed the Fort Worth celebration. Rogers later revealed to friends that Dallas officials, fearing the monetary impact her appearance at Casa Mañana or the Frontier Centennial might have on their coffers, made it a part of her contract that she could not visit the centennial or Fort Worth for thirty days, both before and after her Dallas date.[33]

After the excitement of the opening died down, reporters found themselves forced to come up with new angles for stories. Centennial visitors' comments began appearing weekly in a *Press* column with the alliterative title, "Frontier Flickers." A local archery club challenged Indians appearing in "The Last Frontier" to an impromptu marksmanship contest. The Indians lost—temporarily. Vindication

Six Tiny Rosebuds of Pioneer Palace Revue.

Courtesy Special Collections, UTA.

came a few days later when the warriors resoundingly trounced the pretenders in a rematch, using only dimestore-quality bows and arrows. John Search the Enemy, a seventy-three-year-old Sioux medicine man, died, reportedly after eating raw beef kidneys. Several of Sally Rand's Nude Ranch performers resigned after being spotted by visiting friends and relatives. The vacancies were quickly filled. In the Pioneer Palace the Six Tiny Rosebuds became seven when Mildred Monti, largest of the dancers, gave birth to a six-pound daughter in a local hospital. She had continued in the line until three days before the birth with patrons unaware of her delicate condition.[34]

Other problems developed next door in Casa Mañana. Faye Cotton broke out in a chronic rash from wearing the metallic gown next to her unprotected skin in the heat. Fickle breezes played havoc with Sally Rand's props. At a dress rehearsal shortly before the official opening of the theater, a sudden gust of wind had snatched her balloon camouflage and sent it floating across the tiers of unoccupied tables and chairs. Ordinarily nude, Rand was clothed for the rehearsal. Later, however, the incident reoccurred during an actual performance. Once again the bubble skidded into the audience, depriving her briefly of her cover. Helpful patrons halted the balloon's progress and tossed it back to Rand, who deftly caught it and completed her act without further incident. A third incident had less fortunate results. Once again the balloon escaped, only to be caught by a grinning theater patron holding a lighted cigarette. The balloon disintegrated with a bang. Rand, displaying notable savoir-faire, completed the act anyway.[35]

Through the remainder of the summer, Paul Whiteman continued his regular weekly national broadcasts from the local Ringside Club, with pianist/arranger Roy Bargy opening each session with "Rhapsody In Blue."[36] The total silence required for the broadcasts necessitated shutting off fans and closing most doors and windows despite summer temperatures well into the nineties. Some band members removed jackets and ties for comfort although Whiteman himself seemed oblivious to the heat and always wore an impeccable white suit. On Friday, August 28, no one complained about the temperature as the bands of Whiteman, Joe Venuti, Hyman Maurice, Emile Hollander, and Ed Lally combined to heat up the Casa Mañana stage in a special live two-hour midnight program broadcast from New York to Los Angeles. The event spotlighted stars from all the centennial's major shows, but Sally Rand stole the evening as she and Walter Dere Wahl performed an energetic burlesque of Dere Wahl's regular acrobatic act. With listeners across the country tuned in, the broadcast appropriately opened and closed with "The Eyes of Texas Are Upon You."

Then there were the monkeys. Billy Rose and his architects learned an important lesson in primate behavior: monkeys can swim. Undeterred by the water-filled moat intended to trap them on their private island paradise, the monkeys began conducting lightning raids on centennial exhibits. They drank beer alongside patrons in the Silver Dollar Saloon, dived into the Ziegfeld milk bath, and scurried across Casa Mañana's revolving stage. Centennial photographer Ed Gruber returned to his office one afternoon to discover a foraging party of apes systematically admiring and then destroying pictures of showgirls. Keepers coaxed the mischief makers back to their sanctuary with relative ease until one evening a prankster loaded his car with as many of the creatures as it would hold and headed for downtown Fort Worth. Cornered by police, the jokester released his hairy charges, leaving them free to scurry into the neighborhoods close by the courthouse. Complaints from angry housewives about playing hostess to uninvited dinner guests and clean laundry dragged from clotheslines eventually forced Rose to take action. He created a new staff position, hiring J. R. Brown as permanent monkey chaser.[37]

In early protests lodged against Billy Rose by the local clergy, one of the more notorious critics of Fort Worth vice had been notable for his silence. Throughout the festivities, nationally known evangelist J. Frank Norris remained uncharacteristically quiet. Norris had fomented strife in the Southern Baptist Convention for years until he finally split with that organization and formed his own church. He had acquired a reputation for outspoken and often flamboyant crusading over a career spanning three decades. Because of his large following in Fort Worth, the Frontier Centennial Board feared the damage Norris might cause if he ever met with the press and pronounced Casa Mañana or some of the more lurid of its sideshows unfit for decent citizens. Amon Carter and Norris openly despised each other.[38]

For most of the summer, the board relaxed because Norris providentially stayed away, absent on a cross-country evangelistic campaign. But one evening in September, following his return to Fort Worth, Norris paid an unscheduled visit to Casa Mañana. Word of impending disaster reached the amphitheater only moments before Norris arrived; staff members activated emergency plans designed specifically to confound any disruption of Sally Rand's number. Billy Rose himself approached Norris, who leaned casually against a rail, a calculated study in nonchalance. Just as Rand made her first entrance of the night, Rose engaged Norris in earnest conversation. As added insurance, someone dispatched a waiter with a fake phone summons. The emergency measures may have worked, but more likely, Norris secretly relished the frenzy precipitated by his unannounced arrival. Reporters gathering in anticipation of a bombshell for the early editions received a shock of their own. Norris' comments, uncharacteristically low key, took note of the show's popularity and concluded ambiguously, "My hat is off to Amon Carter and his associates. They've done a real job."[39]

As summer drifted into fall, ongoing problems with financing lessened somewhat as Amon Carter renewed his pressure on the WPA, this time with a telegram to Franklin Roosevelt. Three days later John Nance Garner notified him that the WPA had reversed its original position and would loan the centennial an additional $50,000.[40] Carter, who had a policy against giving free passes to *Star-Telegram* employees even for company-sponsored events, paid his own way into Casa Mañana sixty-five times.[41]

While some of the Frontier Centennial shows with lower overheads than Casa Mañana and *Jumbo* fared better, *Variety* still noted with awe the staggering production costs of the overall exposition, sums that the new loan would do little to cover. The weekly payroll alone for 1,500 employees amounted to $70,000. Casa Mañana, the largest, most elaborate attraction, was also the costliest, with operating expenses of $30,000 a week. Next came *Jumbo* at $16,000, "The Last Frontier" at $6,500, and the Pioneer Palace and Nude Ranch each needing $2,000. In terms of relative value, Sally Rand represented the most expensive single commodity because of her $1,000-a-week paycheck. Originally, when the centennial board had believed that $750,000 of critical operating capital could be raised through bond sales, backers calculated that 1,500,000 paid admissions would put the Frontier Centennial in the black. However, with steadily escalating costs, slow bond sales, and smaller-than-expected revenues, that number was steadily revised upward until the new break-even estimate topped 3,000,000 paying customers. To compensate for the *Jumbo* flop and to help cover losses from other shows, the original weekday price for Casa Mañana tickets went from $1.00 to $1.50, while Saturday admissions climbed to $2.00. Profits took an additional, unexpected hit from customers paying their way into the first performance and then staying on to see the second show. Other patrons complained about having to purchase a meal at "nightclub prices" when all they really wanted was to see the show. In the interim, while show officials grappled with ways to appease dissatisfied patrons and still clear the cabaret between shows, Rose ordered the placing of 1,000 additional chairs for those not interested in dining."[42]

From the centennial's opening, negroes had been barred from the fairgrounds, except for 250 waiters employed in Casa Mañana. Blacks in the community mounted their own exhibition, the "Century of Negro Progress," an event that opened at Lake Como on June 17, two days before the traditional Juneteenth celebration. Only as it became clear that the centennial had little chance of breaking even unless attendance could somehow be boosted, did management begin admitting negroes to *Jumbo* and "The Last Frontier," two shows whose profit margins had steadily declined. *Variety* estimated the potential gain in paying customers at between 35,000 and 40,000 from Fort Worth alone but condescendingly referred to black patrons as the centennial's "Joe Louis gate hypo." Blacks who did attend could enter the grounds only through two side gates and then sat separated from white customers. They remained completely shut out of the more profitable Casa Mañana and Pioneer Palace revues as well as general exhibit areas.[43] Similar inequities victimized black patrons of the main centennial exposition in Dallas. Negroes could enter the grounds, but inside, refreshment vendors either refused to serve them at all or demanded prices inflated to double or triple those charged white customers. Only one building, The Hall of Negro Life, contained restrooms open to black customers—all others were labeled "Whites Only."[44]

Fall brought new problems. The weather worsened with thunderstorms throughout September and October causing performers to lose their footing and fall on the slippery boards of Casa Mañana's stage. Patrons and performers alike shivered as chilling winds blew increasingly from the north. The blonde in the Ziegfeld Milk Bath threatened to quit if she did not get warmer milk. Rose coped with the seasonal climate vagaries by ordering the entire Casa Mañana Revue moved indoors to the smaller *Jumbo* building on the worst evenings. To compensate for the losses in seating, he added additional performances each evening. *Jumbo* itself, done in finally by a combination of heat and poor ventilation, had closed down for good after playing to houses less than two-thirds full from the beginning of the centennial. *Variety* chronicled its demise with the headline, Jumbo Disintegrates Into 50-Cent Circus: Texas Date Another Flop, Ran Show $30,000 Further Into Red.[45] A replacement attempt featuring international circus acts and some of the *Jumbo* performers had no better luck, closing after less than two weeks.

Other changes at Casa Mañana were unrelated to the weather, changes calculated to give performers a break in routine while luring repeat customers back through the cabaret's imposing archways. Paul Whiteman, Sally Rand, and Everett Marshall stayed on as feature attractions, but new acts replaced those performers whose contracts had expired at the end of summer. Additions to the fall lineup included Jack Powell, a comic drummer from Ed Wynn's popular "Laff Parade," mimic Eddie Garr, and Paul Remos and his Wonder Midgets. Sally Rand took over Ann Pennington's "Little Egypt" number, and Pennington began appearing in a dance duet with Tom Patricola, one of her former dancing partners from the Scandals and Ziegfeld Follies. If Billy Rose harbored secret concerns over sagging revenues or attendance, there were no visible signs on the centennial grounds. The fun continued, seemingly unabated, and the show, originally scheduled to close October 31, had its run extended to November 14. Casa Mañana finished the last two weeks of its season with extra performances added on weekend evenings to handle the demand for seats but without the services of Paul Whiteman and Sally Rand. Whiteman, whose contract extended only through the original October closing, had other commitments which precluded his continued stay in Fort Worth. He left regretfully, promising to return at the earliest possible date.[46]

Sally Rand once again became the focus of a controversy after Billy Rose discovered that she had hired ten of his most attractive Casa Mañana dancers for her own "Texas All-Star Revue." Maintaining she had no idea that Casa Mañana would be extended beyond the originally scheduled closing date, Rand quit on schedule at the end of her contract period, taking the girls with her. On Sunday night, November 1, in an open challenge to Rose, Rand appeared at the centennial gates flashing her engraved centennial pass, all ten girls bringing up the rear. Someone had evidently anticipated the maneuver, and the gatekeeper apologetically confiscated the pass, explaining he had orders from "higher ups." Undeterred, Rand gleefully purchased eleven tickets to the evening's first show and led her entourage to prime ringside tables. One of the dancers vividly recalled the battle of egos that took place: "Billy was really mad that we left because Sally took some of his best dancers and showgirls, but the show was going to close anyway. It made him so mad, [that Sally] took us all to see the show. We sat on the front row, watched everybody perform, and clapped." In a move calculated more to frighten the less sophisticated teenage members of the party than to intimidate Rand, a blustering Rose accused the ten girls of violating their contracts. "He said we'd never work for him again," remembered dancer Wilby Lingo. By the next season he backed down from his threats and rehired all the girls.[47]

On November 14, 1936, Casa Mañana and the Frontier Centennial finally concluded its run, although in reality the last performance did not end until 12:10 A.M on November 15. The show begun as a long shot had outlasted its detractors and brought national prominence to Billy Rose and to Fort Worth. The hard financial reality that Casa Mañana had little hope of recouping its enormous production costs paled in comparison to the positive impact of the event on the economy and morale of the community. For Fort Worth, which had taken Casa Mañana to its heart, and for many of the performers as well, the closing had a far more personal and sentimental impact. Letting go proved difficult. Local newspapers continued to carry stories and pictures of teary farewells for days after the final strains of "The Night Is Young and You're So Beautiful" had faded. At one of the celebratory parties after Casa Mañana's final performance, Will Morrisey, Billy Rose's personal representative, distilled the sentiments of many when he versified,

> "We are leaving Heaven, going back to earth,
> But gosh we're going to miss Fort Worth."[48]

IT CAN'T HAPPEN HERE

The Frontier Centennial of 1936 lost $97,000—hardly a staggering sum, but in the Depression the amount represented a sizable loss. A financial report made public in early 1937 revealed that the Fort Worth Centennial Exhibition cost $1,509,000, of which only $1,122,375 had been furnished by loans or subscriptions. Throughout the entire summer and fall, the centennial made only $289,000—all other expenses had to be underwritten. Thirty-eight firms and individuals provided over sixty percent of operating costs. Of these the largest single investor other than banks was Amon Carter's *Fort Worth Star-Telegram* which contributed $58,450.[1]

Few seemed to mind the losses. Fort Worth continued to bask in the afterglow of Casa Mañana and the Frontier Centennial for months. To an appreciation dinner given for the centennial board, Billy Rose wired, "This is the first time I have ever heard of a city giving an appreciation dinner to a group for losing eleven hundred thousand dollars of their money. Usually, exposition directors have to leave town by the dark of the moon." Rose himself could not attend the dinner because his mother had been hospitalized with heart problems. She died on December 9, 1936. James North, editor of the *Star-Telegram*, reported that even William Monnig came around. Years later Monnig admitted, "Fort Worth was flat on its back until we put on that show. Then it started growing and it has been growing ever since." But he was also fond of grumbling, "We paid Billy Rose too much money. We were suckers to pay him that $100,000.[2]

As 1936 drew to a close, one fact still seemed inescapable: Fort Worth was not ready to let go of Casa Mañana. Bing Crosby sang "The Night Is Young and

You're So Beautiful" to his national radio audience, making one critical error. To the outrage of hometowners, Crosby attributed the song's origin to the Dallas Centennial Exposition. Local newspapers wistfully followed the doings of Casa Mañana stars as each drifted on to other shows in other cities. The Canovas and the Six Tiny Rosebuds sent Christmas greetings to local admirers and spoke of how much they missed Cowtown. Paul Whiteman and his band returned in early 1937 for a concert at the Lake Worth Casino benefitting the Milk and Ice Fund. Whiteman recalled fondly to local reporter Robert Randol that during his 1936 sojourn at Casa Mañana he had collected a set of ivory-handled Colt .45s, a pair of gold spurs, a leather vest, leather chaps, five horses, an oversized cowboy hat, and a spread of his own on Eagle Mountain Lake.[3] Initially reluctant to accept the engagement at Casa Mañana, he never forgot the genuineness of Texans or the affection lavished on him. At a testimonial dinner given in his honor at the

Early arrivals to Casa Mañana await the start of dinner on opening night, July 18, 1936.

Courtesy Fort Worth Public Library.

The Black Horse Troop of the
Second United States Cavalry,
costumed in authentic uniforms
of nineteenth-century Dragoons,
pose with performers and Indian
tribesmen appearing in "The Last
Frontier."

Courtesy Special Collections, UTA.

Fort Worth Club shortly before his departure, Whiteman spoke movingly of his experiences: "I am a Texan because you made me one of you. I came down here sorely in need of spiritual uplift. In Texas I have found it." Saying he was "mentally and physically at a low ebb," he continued,

> I have learned the real meaning of the words "friend and neighbor." And I have received a strength of mind and uplift of spirit which will go with me the rest of my days. I am bound to Texas by irrevocable ties. . . .[4]

Through the winter, the show grounds remained deserted and boarded up, abandoned except for a solitary caretaker and a scrawny cat that took up residence in the *Jumbo* building. Billy Rose, as a direct result of his Casa Mañana triumph and then in lieu of any promising movie deals, had moved on to Cleveland, in the second year of its Great Lakes Exposition. Photographers snapped him in the company of Olympic gold medalist Eleanor Holm, attractive swimming star of his newest extravaganza billed as an "Aquacade." Both parties denied persistent rumors linking them romantically, but reporters remained hopeful.

Popular bandleader Paul
Whiteman and his wife during a
visit to Amon Carter's Shady
Oak Ranch. During his stay in
Fort Worth, Whiteman collected
five horses, a pair of Colt .45s,
gold spurs, leather chaps embla-
zoned "Mr. P.W.," and land on
Eagle Mountain Lake.

Courtesy Special Collections, UTA.

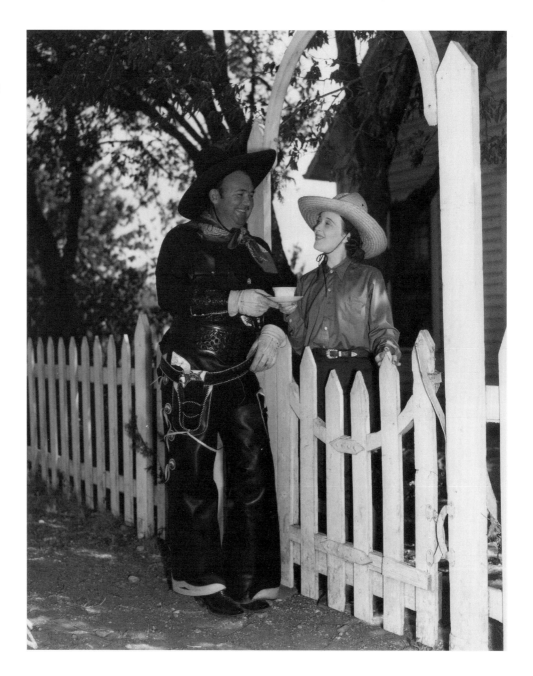

Several parallels existed between the Cleveland and Fort Worth shows.
Both had opened in 1936, although the Great Lakes Exposition, with its much
larger 135-acre lakefront showground had been conceived as a permanent urban
renewal project.[5] And both, despite good first-year attendance, lost money due
largely to startup construction costs. Finally, both cities were now counting on
Billy Rose to move them beyond the second-year doldrums that traditionally
plagued similar exhibitions with previous season deficits to overcome.

The Cleveland Great Lakes Exposition featured the huge stage of Casa Mañana all over again—except that this "stage," in the form of a 128-foot barge flanked by two sixty-five-foot diving towers, was fabricated in a local shipyard and then towed to its exposition berth just offshore on the waters of Lake Erie. Underwater nozzles provided a forty-foot "water curtain," and at show's end each evening, the stage moved in, allowing the audience to dance to the orchestra. The Aquacade chorus consisted of several dozen synchronized swimmers, dubbed "Aquabelles" by Rose. He christened Eleanor Holm "Aquabelle Number One" and her co-star, Olympic swimmer Johnny Weissmuller, "Aquadonis Number One."[6] Jack Gordon flew to Cleveland to satisfy his own and his readers' curiosity; he reported back, "I'm convinced Mr. Rose has moved everything but the mortgage up from the Fort Worth Centennial." Many of the same acts, musical numbers, and entertainers also appeared, albeit in different costumes; many of the creations designed for the Fort Worth exposition by Brooks Costumes had also moved to Cleveland. There was even a Pioneer Palace, complete with Tom Patricola, Lulu Bates, and the Six Tiny Rosebuds. Rose was simply continuing to demonstrate his flair for identifying popular venues and then appropriating the most consistent moneymakers for his own purposes, a talent destined to embroil him in controversy before year's end.[7]

Despite continuing obligations in Cleveland, by March of 1937 Rose announced his early return to Fort Worth to stage an all-new version of Casa Mañana and the Frontier Centennial. He vowed, "We'll be all-American, not Pan-American," a reference to Dallas' new show for 1937, the Pan-American Exposition. With the centennial year over, Fort Worth planners announced a similar name change for the local exhibition—from Frontier Centennial to Frontier Fiesta.

Rose scoffed at Dallas plans to build an outdoor theater with sliding glass roof to protect spectators in case of showers, claiming such a theater could never hope to see a profit or pay back the expense of construction. As predicted, the Dallas theater never materialized, but the fact that planners even considered such a design paid tribute to the notice Casa Mañana received. Miami, Cleveland, and Atlanta all announced their own plans to build a Casa Mañana.[8]

The losses incurred in the previous season as well as the fact that a complete showground now awaited any new production probably contributed to an announced salary cut for Rose in 1937—a relatively paltry $50,000, plus a percentage of any profits. Other than this change, however, the 1937 Casa Mañana began to sound suspiciously like 1936. Most of the 1936 production staff returned with Rose—John Murray Anderson, Raoul Pène du Bois, Albert Johnson, Dana Suesse, Carlton Winckler, and Robert Alton all signed on. Rose also launched a statewide search for a new "Texas Sweetheart Number One" of 1937. The search culminated on June 5 with the selection of Grey Downs of Temple. Rose also announced all new auditions for at least 100 showgirls and dancers, although this time promising to use all local talent—nothing imported from New York.

The announcement of auditions for the 1937 Casa Mañana precipitated a rush both of newcomers and seasoned showgirls from the 1936 revue. Competition for a spot in the cast matched the intensity of the 1936 campaign. Former showgirls, eager to regain old jobs, besieged Billy Rose with phone calls; he decreed, Solomon-like, that all comers had to reapply. For the second year in a row, several hundred aspiring dancers and actresses converged on Fort Worth from across the state to brave the sarcasm, withering scrutiny, and exacting standards of John Murray Anderson. One New York showgirl, Marjorie Groffel, a redhead younger than some of the other New York dancers, became distraught over Rose's earlier vow to use only local talent.[9] She pleaded with Rose to reconsider, explaining she had the best of reasons for needing a job in Fort Worth: she was engaged to a local boy, Dominique Childs. The two had met during the 1936 revue when both worked as dancers, she in Casa Mañana and he in "The Last Frontier." At the close of the 1936 season, Groffel returned to New York and home, but the persistent Childs followed her. Rose eventually took pity on the lovers and reinstated Groffel, making her the only member of the Casa Mañana ensemble from New York.[10]

Rejected at one session as unsuitable, some of the more determined auditioners simply returned the next day in different costume. Inevitably, Murray Anderson spied the interlopers, dismissing them with a blunt, "You just won't do—there isn't a possibility for you to get in."[11] This scrupulous attention to the presentation of the female form prompted one *Fort Worth Press* reader to observe, "For 40 years West Texans have been coming to see the cows at the Fat Stock Show. Now twice as many come to see calves—in Casa Mañana."[12]

Rose's sober pronouncement that all comers must audition sometimes produced comical situations. A man showed up on the grounds claiming he could dive off a 100-foot tower into a bucket of sawdust. Rose refused to hire him unless he jumped. The man agreed, equipment was set up, and he dived.

"You're hired," said Rose.

The daredevil hesitated. "I'm very sorry, Mr. Rose, but I decline."

"Why?" asked Rose.

"I've got a headache," the gentleman replied, going on to admit that he had never attempted the stunt before.[13]

Everett Marshall and Paul Whiteman signed early to reprise their performances in 1937. The only new faces in the 1937 show came from the community of Fort Worth. Heading up the campaign to raise the necessary funds for the 1937 show was businessman Ben E. Keith, with James F. Pollock designated show manager and Boyce House, publicity manager. In the midst of Prohibition, Keith had parlayed a beer distributorship into a highly successful local wholesale firm, the Ben E. Keith Company. He, like Amon Carter, was a tireless booster of Fort Worth and Texas.[14] Succeeding William Monnig as president of the new Frontier Fiesta Board was Will K. Stripling. The Stripling family, like Monnig and his brothers, had played a prominent role in the mercantile history of Fort Worth. W. C. Stripling had brought Stripling's Department Store to the city in 1893 after previously opening stores in Alvord and Bowie. With the elder Stripling's death in 1934, son Will assumed control of the family business. During the 1920s the younger Stripling gained experience serving as president of the Fort Worth Cats baseball team in a period when the team won six consecutive Texas League championships.[15]

In contrast to the campaign of 1936, Billy Rose maintained that the 1937 Casa Mañana would be kept on an "intellectual plane." The scenario he presented to the Chamber of Commerce called for staging scenes from four best-selling novels: *Gone With the Wind*, *Wake Up and Live*, *Lost Horizon*, and

It Can't Happen Here.[16] Rose intended to feature ballerina Harriet Hoctor in what he promised would be a "huge ballet sequence." Styled the "Pavlova of America" by showman Florenz Ziegfeld after the legendary Russian ballerina, Anna Pavlova, Hoctor had appeared in the Ziegfeld Follies and in the movies *Shall We Dance*, alongside Fred Astaire and Ginger Rogers, and *The Great Ziegfeld*.

Superficially, at least, the 1937 Casa Mañana Revue had acquired "culture" through its literary connections; Rose, more than likely, had something else in mind entirely. As part of his ongoing "educational" strategy, he revealed negotiations with Gypsy Rose Lee, "Queen of the Strippers," to present an act with the specious billing, "The Evolution of the Strip-Tease." Rose wired Lee offering her "three G's" to appear. She fired back, "Do you mean three strings or grands? Answer."[17] Lee never appeared but important changes occurring in the professional theater suggest that Rose, more cabaret showman than "legitimate" producer, may have hoped to capitalize on the success of an ongoing experiment aimed at reviving the severely depressed legitimate stage world of the mid-1930s.

In 1935, WPA director Harry Hopkins appointed Hallie Flanagan, director of the Vassar Experimental Theater, to head the newly organized Federal Theater Project (FTP). Her mission was to provide projects and employment to thousands of professional actors, stagehands, technicians, and musicians left jobless by a dual blow: competition from motion pictures and the generally bleak economics of the era. By the end of 1932, a majority of Broadway theaters had closed their doors. Franklin and Eleanor Roosevelt took a personal interest in the plight of theater personnel, because a federally administered series of theatrical projects to provide entertainment and education to small and remote communities had long been a favorite interest of the Roosevelts. With the support of Hopkins and the Roosevelts, Flanagan set out to recruit major artists, writers, and directors. Despite active opposition from anti-Roosevelt segments of Congress and the press, by December 1935 the project could report 3,350 workers back on the boards. Nonetheless, first efforts were tentative, plagued by regional disputes and attempts at censorship and largely isolated from audiences outside New York. In 1936 the effort received a singular boost when Pulitzer Prize-winning author

Sinclair Lewis chose the FTP over other commercial Broadway interests to stage his 1935 novel, *It Can't Happen Here*, the story of a fascist dictatorship seizing control of American government from within. In a bold stroke, the FTP coordinated twenty-two separate productions of the novel in theaters across the country, opening them simultaneously on October 27, 1936. While critics generally questioned Lewis' abilities as a dramatist, Brooks Atkinson, writing in the *New York Times* observed, "*It Can't Happen Here* ought to scare the daylights out of the heedless American who believes as this column does, that it can't happen here as long as Mr. Lewis keeps his health."[18] Despite its detractors, the play's story and theme evidently tapped fears already simmering in the nation's collective conscious. Before the productions' close four months later, the combined stagings had played in English, Yiddish, and Spanish to nearly 500,000 people for a "season" equivalent to a five-year Broadway run.[19] The show's success undoubtedly attracted the attention of producers and theater managers outside the FTP. Burns Mantle, in his syndicated column for the *Chicago Tribune* noted,

> Boston was quite excited by it, one thousand being present and three hundred turned away. Cleveland's capacity audience shuddered a bit, but recovered and gave the actors nine curtain calls. Tacoma accepted the production as an "important and significant event." Detroit thought it dignified and worthwhile and Chicago, we hear, took it in its critical stride, but reported audience reaction as being definitely and noisily in the play's favor.[20]

Billy Rose's staff laid plans for a new production number based on the novel, complete with Roseian trademark pageantry and showgirls and, significantly, placed it as the grand finale in both Cleveland and Fort Worth.[21]

To coordinate with the second-year opening of Casa Mañana, the Fair Department Store and the Woman's Club staged a program of book reviews with several prominent local citizens as presenters. Rose and the ladies, in unlikely partnership, evidently underestimated the public appeal of a good book review—the Crystal Ballroom of the Hotel Texas filled to capacity, and a thousand or so bibliophiles had to be turned away. For those privileged to get a seat, Mrs. L. M. Hogsett set the tone for the day, asserting that Dorothea Brande's *Wake Up and*

Live lent itself ideally "to acceleration of tempo of music and dance." The Reverend Perry E. Gresham searched out angles left unexplored by author Sinclair Lewis in *It Can't Happen Here* through "the opportunity it offers the showman."[22] That the somber Lewis ever envisioned Casa Mañana with its leggy showgirls and chorines as a vehicle for his problematic literary work seems open to debate.

A *Press* reporter prowling the cavernous backstage area of Casa Mañana discovered the $5,000 "gold" gown of Faye Cotton tossed in the corner of a dressing room. The dress, actually fashioned of bronze mesh, had outlived its usefulness as a source of publicity and been unceremoniously discarded. Jack Gordon commented wryly that the dress "probably [would] be melted down to make a chain for the wash room of some battleship."[23] Following the publicity shenanigans of the 1936 season, no one seemed particularly surprised at the discovery. The 1937 campaign, meanwhile, was shaping up as no less eccentric than 1936. Local newspapers weekly traced the progress of the "Billy Rose Clipper," a miniature Conestoga wagon pulled by Edward L. Lark of Fort Worth and on its way, for no clear reason, across the country to New York City. A local radio station sponsored a contest to find the oldest unmarried couple in Tarrant County with the champs, Mrs. Nanny Nicholson, 92, and her beau, Pat Davey, 96, receiving tickets to Casa Mañana. The *Star-Telegram* meanwhile began a quest for the person who had attended Casa Mañana the greatest number of times in 1936. L. A. Eberhart seemed assured of victory in the early tallies with twenty-six visits, but Frank J. Wren eventually claimed the record by offering proof of thirty-two return trips to the outdoor cafe theater.[24]

Ned Alvord also returned, bringing his peculiar talent for alliterative hyperbole. The new 1937 ads, plastered once again on strategic barns and filling stations all over the state, boasted of "200 Alluring Adolescent Aphrodites," and pictured Mary "Stutterin' Sam" Dowell dressed as the "Symbol of Peace." In the background, inexplicably, appeared exotically clad harem girls being burned at the stake. Another ad, capitalizing on the "classical" beauty of Casa Mañana dancers, featured Billy Rose playfully rejecting the Venus de Milo. A war of sorts developed between ad crews from the Frontier Fiesta and the Dallas Pan-American Exposition. After receiving word that rival Pan-American workers had plastered over Fort Worth's billboards in the Dallas area, Alvord instructed Fiesta personnel to replace the offending ads and to coat the new ones with lard to stymie further attempts at sabotage.[25]

For the 1937 Casa Mañana Revue, Rose again enlisted an impressive array of supporting players as backup for stars Everett Marshall and Harriet Hoctor. Larry Lee and his orchestra, hired to fill Casa's second bandstand, assisted Paul Whiteman's musicians in providing dance music for theatergoers. Other acts accorded feature billing included the Calgary Brothers, a team of comic acrobats, Japanese exotic "idol dancers" Sanami and Michi, and Paul Seidel and his trained Chihuahua, Spotty. For reasons only he understood, Rose inserted the canine act into the elaborate "Lost Horizon" sequence.

For "Gone With the Wind," Rose found the Cabin Kids, five black youngsters, actually members of the same family: Ruth Hall, twelve; Helen, eleven; James, nine; Winifred, seven; and Frederick, or "Honey," six. The children, who

Featured performers of 1937 "Gone With the Wind" sequence, the Cabin Kids—Ruth, Helen, James, Winifred and Frederick Hall.

Courtesy Fort Worth Public Library.

traveled with their stepmother, Beatrice Hall, had used their early experiences singing in church to build a successful career in motion pictures, including Bing Crosby's *Mississippi*. At Casa Mañana the youthful ensemble regaled audiences each evening with renditions of "Ezekiel Saw the Wheel," and "Shortnin' Bread," as well as the antics of six-year-old Frederick, who, as part of the act, refused to be kissed by his older sisters. The local press, in the casual racism of the era, referred to the family euphemistically as "pickaninnies" and "musical pickaninnies." An incident further reflecting the prevailing ambivalence in racial tolerance occurred when the downtown Kiwanis Club invited the children to perform at its regular weekly luncheon in the Hotel Texas. As the group and their mother entered the hotel's main lobby, the manager stepped forward and brusquely ordered everyone to detour through a rear door to the freight elevator. Outraged, Hall took the children and left the hotel. Later the Junior Chamber of Commerce asked the singing group to perform in the Blackstone Hotel. Once again, hotel management ordered the family to a rear entrance, and once again Hall walked out on puzzled business leaders.[26]

Other acts featured in the 1937 lineup included Moore and Revel, who burlesqued the elegant adagio style popularized by such dance teams as Fred Astaire and Ginger Rogers; the Stuart Morgan Dancers, three men and a woman, who combined dance with acrobatic leaps and catches. Returning also from the 1936 show were crowd favorites, The Californians. Over the winter the male octet had undergone another name change to become the California Varsity Eight.

Rose needed more than just specialty acts and pretty girls if he hoped to avoid the traditional jinx of sequels and second-year openings. Without the publicity potential of a Sally Rand, he turned instead to pageantry with the focus on sets worthy in scale of a Roman circus and the sumptuous and exotic costume designs of Raoul Pène du Bois. Brooks Costumes once again designed and constructed costumes from its Fort Worth office in Monnig's Main Street warehouse. The demands of creating over 700 costumes necessitated hiring over 200 local seamstresses. More than 200,000 yards of material went into creations often so intricately detailed that much of the work had to be done by hand. Women worked for days trimming southern antebellum ball gowns with scores of handmade roses and pleating skirts for dresses made of silver lamé and cellophane glass. The most spectacular creation by far was the white satin gown worn by the Symbol of Peace in "It Can't Happen Here." The cape alone, seventy-five feet long and sixty-five feet wide, contained over 500 square yards of diaphanous material and 200 yards of hand-appliqued sequins. The costume, requiring the labor of fifteen seamstresses, took nearly a month to complete.[27]

Sally Rand and her fans, featured attraction of the 1936 Casa Mañana Revue. For her Fort Worth appearance, Rand switched to an oversize balloon.

Courtesy New York Public Library.

SALLY RAND

1477-83

Showgirls in the finale of Casa Mañana, 1937, "It Can't Happen Here."

Courtesy Special Collections, UTA.

The 1937 ads portraying Casa Mañana as "Still the World's Largest Dine-Dance Theater" were modestly understated. Each new set was seemingly designed to surpass its predecessor in sometimes outlandish splendor and sheer gigantism. "Gone With the Wind" anticipated its later movie cousin with a full recreation of a southern antebellum mansion fronted by nine white columns twenty-six feet tall. *Variety* termed it "one of the most spacious edifices ever to crowd a stage. Its façade must stretch across a good 200 feet, and it towers up a full three stories." As the stage revolved, the structure burst into flame, an effect achieved by the burning of yellow sulfur. Pipes concealed backstage channeled the smoke through the various windows of the mansion.[28]

"Gone With the Wind" featured Harriet Hoctor as Margaret Mitchell's fickle heroine, Scarlett O'Hara, and Everett Marshall as Scarlett's long-suffering sweetheart, Rhett Butler. The episode itself was a curious blending of styles, tailored to fit the talents of the featured performers rather than to maintain accuracy to Mitchell's novel. As garden party guests whirled in antebellum costumes

Ballerina Harriet Hoctor played Scarlett O'Hara in 1937 "Gone With the Wind" sequence at Casa Mañana.

Courtesy Special Collections, UTA.

to a furious polka, Harriet Hoctor swept in wearing a bright pink dress and toe shoes, leading *Variety* to observe dryly, ". . . in a few minutes on her toes [Hoctor] wipes out a good 600 pages of the original work." The Cabin Kids abetted the cliché with renditions of "negro" songs, and Everett Marshall appeared in time to sing "Gone With the Dawn," a tune constantly touted by Rose as an even bigger hit than the previous summer's "The Night Is Young and You're So Beautiful."

In the revue's second episode, "Lost Horizon," theatergoers marveled at the visual splendor of a Tibetan lamasery, its shimmering façade rising above the stage flanked by two massive bronze chortens or shrines. Three silver gongs suspended from a balcony sounded in unison, adding to the exotic atmosphere of the scene. One critic characterized the sight as "fantastic, impossible and beautiful." Against this lush backdrop, Rose introduced another Ziegfeld display of showgirls rivaling his Parisian scene of 1936.[29]

This "Oriental Dress Parade" included Casa Mañana showgirls daringly garbed in costumes amounting to little more than "two scant pieces of gold, with trains of vivid yellow caught up in a puff behind [with] sweeping gold peacocks standing out from their left ears."[30] Sanami and Michi led the brilliant-hued procession, carried on in a ten-foot birdcage by four brawny Casa Mañana showboys, actually members of the TCU football squad.

Of the four scenes presented, "Wake Up and Live" earned the least interest from the press. *Variety* rated the scene's signature number, "Live the Life of Your Dreams," "not so hot," while still calling Harriet Hoctor's dancing and the Calgary Brothers clowning "top notch."[31] Against a backdrop clearly reminiscent of New York's Central Park and Casino, a tramp snoozed on a park bench while dancers attired in velvet riding habits "trotted" about on large hobbyhorses conveniently equipped with wheels. The scene had been choreographed more elaborately, but the horse props proved too unwieldy for the petite dancers. Olive Nicolson remembered, "They had planned to have us do a lot of things, but when they got [the horses] made up, they were so heavy we could hardly move. We'd kind of walk across and the boys would hold them [up]."[32] Moore and Revel clowned through a ballroom dance number, and the California

Varsity Eight sang "I Haven't Got the Girl" to Grey Downs, "Texas Sweetheart Number One" of 1937.

The show's finale blatantly mixed spectacle with politics in a gaudy representation of *It Can't Happen Here*, a scene clearly intended to capitalize on the national paranoia over the spread of totalitarianism in Europe. *Texas Weekly* termed the resulting concoction "a futuristic description of democracy which is so patriotic that it narrowly escapes chauvinism."[33] As the stage revolved to open the scene, Everett Marshall solemnly intoned,

> In Europe there are black shirts, brown shirts, red
> shirts—madness, revolution, chaos—but here in
> America there is peace. If we can guard our own
> backyard "It Can't Happen Here." [34]

Waving huge banners symbolizing fascism, nazism, and communism, armies wearing black shirts, brown shirts, and red shirts clashed in mock battle across the 130-foot expanse of the stage. American involvement in World War II still lay over four years away, yet growing political tensions in Europe lent the tableau a tone of somber reality somewhat out of keeping with the lightweight subject matter of the revue's earlier sequences. Rose himself, in comments made before the Chamber of Commerce, described the finale as "completely in the spirit of the times."[35]

The scene's denouement, however, was pure Roseian grandiosity. Costumed as America's Forces of the Land, Forces of the Air, and Forces of the Sea, the Casa Mañana ensemble massed to engulf the forces of political darkness and oppression in a silver and white patent-leather display of nationalistic fervor and military superiority. An overwhelmed John Rosenfield, amusements editor of the *Dallas Morning News*, described the climactic moments:

> Everything previously known in Casa Mañana and as far as we know, in all
> show business is topped by the finale with the entire corps marching from
> the floor up countless chromium steps to the sky. As if this edifice were not
> tall enough, elevators shoot boys and girls still higher and higher. This is
> without a doubt, the most complete overpowering of the senses that a
> revue producer has ever devised.[36]

"It Can't Happen Here," grand finale of 1937 Casa Mañana "Best Sellers" revue featuring showgirl Mary Dowell as the "Symbol of Peace." The massive train of Dowell's costume contained 500 square yards of material.

Courtesy Texas/Dallas History and Archives Division, Dallas Public Library. Hereinafter Dallas Public Library.

Variety applauded the segment, calling it "strictly hokum in spades—but a peach." Four miniature battleships steamed into the lagoon firing their cannons, showers of fireworks exploded, and the flags of Texas and the United States rose majestically atop a fifty-foot flagpole. The bands of Whiteman and Lee played "The Stars and Stripes Forever," and in the scene's crowning moment, the Symbol of Peace, portrayed by Mary Dowell, ascended the four-story staircase, her white satin gown framed by a ten-foot pair of white wings. As she approached the top, twenty-four train bearers extended the gown's cape until it completely covered the full expanse of the gargantuan set. The combined weight of the train and wings was so great that Dowell had to wear specially designed iron shoulder braces. Even with the braces the crushing weight of the costume often reduced her to tears by the end of each evening's two performances.[37]

The scene presented other unique problems in staging. The vast set, weighing nine tons and pieced together in eleven sections like a massive jigsaw puzzle, required forty skilled stagehands to maneuver it into position. The entire operation had to be completed in less than twelve minutes. The mid-scene transformation from fascist to American costume produced additional havoc. Ensemble members repeatedly entered with trousers on backward, shoes that did not match, and unbuttoned tunics. John Murray Anderson threatened the cast, "We're going to stay out here all night until you can make the change," but, after several marathon sessions, he was temporarily forced to accept defeat. Following the show's press preview on June 25, he ordered the elimination of opening battle scenes for several days until dancers could execute the change from fascist black to the silver of American aviators in less than fifty seconds.[38] As if Anderson did not have enough problems to solve already, the closing fireworks display was canceled by order of the fire marshall after exploding rockets set a nearby food tent ablaze. Damage was estimated at $50.

Other 1937 fiesta shows, while less exotic in their offerings, delivered a diverse and sometimes bizarre assortment of attractions. In the former Wild West pavilion "Flirting With Death" replaced "The Last Frontier" with a series of acts that boasted "the most icy-nerved conglomeration of death defying performers ever collected in one ring." The circus-type daredevil acts included "Babcock the Great," a woman motorcyclist inside a gold ball, another cyclist who looped the loop, an Annie Oakley-style markswoman, three acrobats who performed on a platform fifty-five feet above the crowd, and Manuel King, a twelve-year-old lion tamer from Brownsville, Texas. Ushers in grotesque red costumes dominated by a skull and crossbones pattern greeted show patrons. Light in a garish shade of green bathed the entire arena, contributing even further to the macabre atmosphere. Despite the show's sensational overtones, most acts came off without incident, with the possible exception of that of Galen Gough.

Gough, who billed himself as "The Strongest Man on Earth," had suffered severe head injuries during his service with the Marines in World War I, injuries which left him partially paralyzed. He claimed to have cured himself through a strict regimen of crude isometrics that he created for himself, a cure so complete that it led to a new career in show business. Among his other accomplishments, Gough had once dangled beneath an airplane, gripping a rope with nothing but his teeth, as the plane circled the Washington Monument.[39] In his signature act, a stunt he had performed over a thousand times since the 1920s, Gough lay on his back as a six-ton truck rolled over his body. One evening early in the run of the show, the strong man was knocked unconscious during the first performance. For the second show, he reappeared, bruised and shaken but determined to finish the act. He boasted to the crowd, "I'm the only man in the world who lets a truck run over him. I'll do it until I'm finished." Gough's claim very nearly became self-fulfilling prophecy. He attempted to compensate for the earlier injuries, including a large bruise on his back, by lying on his stomach. The move proved to be ill-advised. A slight twist of the wheels by an inexperienced driver, and Gough failed to rise after the truck's second pass. Ambulance attendants carried him gingerly out of the arena and took him to St. Joseph Hospital, where doctors at first diagnosed Gough's injuries as a severe sprain. A week later though they revised the original diagnosis. Gough had suffered a crushed pelvis, his first disabling injury in seventeen years of performing the same act. By mutual consent, Gough and Rose agreed to terminate his contract.[40]

The "Honky Tonk Review" in the Pioneer Palace was missing the Six Tiny Rosebuds, who had moved on to Billy Rose's new show in Cleveland. Filling their ample shoes were early "talkie" singing star Charles King, female vocalist Janet Reade, Clyde Hager, billed as a "comic hawker of potato peelers," and vaudeville hoofer Pat Rooney, Jr. W. C. Fields had once said of Rooney, "If you didn't hear the taps you would think he was floating over the stage." His best-known routine was "The Daughter of Rosie O'Grady," done with trousers hitched up, hands in pockets, and an impish grin on his face. In Fort Worth he performed a precision dance routine with his son Pat Rooney, III. Replacing what one critic termed "the slovenly" Nude Ranch concession, crews demolished the entire midway area to make way for "Firefly Garden" where the Salici Marionettes performed amid seventy-two freshly transplanted hackberry trees sparkling with 10,000 tiny lights.[41] Rose also decreed that he would allow no fortune-tellers on the fiesta grounds. Asked to elaborate he explained, "[they] can tell you everything about the future except whether they'll be working."[42]

In the *Jumbo* building, Rose instituted what was to become a common piece in all of his future theatrical enterprises—a nostalgic trip into the past via performers of yesteryear. In 1937, Rose applied the formula to "Melody Lane," which showcased eight composers and their best-known tunes. Among those featured were David Guion, popularizer of "Home On the Range"; Ernie Burnett, author of "Melancholy Baby"; Euday Bowman, composer of "Twelfth Street Rag"; Joe Howard, who penned "I Wonder Who's Kissing Her Now"; and Harry Armstrong, creator of "Sweet Adeline."[43]

On June 24th Jack Gordon reported chilly weather crippling attendance at the Cleveland Aquacade. In its first season nearly four million saw the exposition, and in 1937 financial backers, bolstered with the talents of Billy Rose, expected to boost that figure to five million. In fact, the unseasonal rain and cold persisted throughout the month of June, sharply cutting attendance and profits.[44] Dallas officials, meanwhile, publicly berated locals for not supporting the Pan-American Exposition. But while Cleveland and Dallas shivered and steamed respectively, the first two shows of Casa Mañana sold out and Rose consoled himself over his Cleveland losses by adding a third performance in Fort Worth. *Variety* predicted, "Billy Rose has produced a show which is not only colossal, gigantic, but which should turn in a healthy profit."[45] Dana Suesse and Everett Marshall received invitations from Washington, D.C., to dinner at the White House. Afterward they regaled the Roosevelts with songs from both the 1936 and the 1937 Casa Mañana revues. On opening day, June 26, in a reprise of his own performance from the previous summer, President Franklin Roosevelt once again electronically cut the lariat to open the 1937 Frontier Fiesta by pushing a button from aboard the presidential yacht, *Sewanna*, anchored in Chesapeake Bay. Over 12,000 persons attended opening night performances of Casa Mañana, and for much of the summer, the theater was filled to capacity or near every night. On July 4, the largest crowd in the two seasons swirled through the gates, surpassing attendance records set during the centennial year. [46]

"THE FOLD OF FOLDS"

Billy Rose, after years of languishing in the shadow of his famous wife, had what he had always wanted. He was courted and lionized across the nation. Following the dual premieres of the Aquacade and Frontier Fiesta, one reporter exulted, "Rose is so good he competes only with Rose."[1] John Rosenfield, still reeling from the titanic spectacle of "It Can't Happen Here," and "Lost Horizon" proclaimed, "After all is said and done, the Fort Worth Fiesta *is* the Casa Mañana, the square of all the bigness hitherto known in the living theater." While acknowledging continuing technical difficulties, he attributed this to the show's massiveness and concluded, "When Mr. Rose's professional staff finishes tinkering Fort Worth will boast of the second wonder of the entertainment world."[2] *Life* featured the producer and the two open-air revues in a multi-page layout in mid-July, tracing the ups and downs of Rose's career from his humble beginnings on New York's lower East Side. Calling him "a little man with a Napoleonic penchant for the colossal and magnificent," the magazine proclaimed Rose "the country's number one purveyor of mass entertainment."[3] After years of relative obscurity, Rose suddenly personified the show business "overnight success."

Following the June 26 opening of Casa Mañana and the Frontier Fiesta, Rose shuttled almost weekly between Hollywood, Fort Worth, and Cleveland. Rumors persisted of big movie deals in the works and a purported romance with his beautiful Aquacade star, Eleanor Holm. He staunchly denied the reports, saying, "The only time I've been near divorce was when Fanny had to stand thirty minutes to get a seat on opening night at Casa Mañana."[4] Rose also announced plans for a new revue to be called "Billy Rose's Show of Shows." He described the project as an "autobiographical production" featuring excerpts from *Jumbo*, Casa Mañana, Aquacade, Pioneer Palace, and other Rose "greatest hits." Rose immediately began signing male and female dancers from Casa Mañana to appear in the revue, which he intended to try out in Brownwood, move then to Fort Worth, and finally to the West Coast.[5]

In 1937, lacking the box office gold mine of a Sally Rand, Rose evidently perceived fresh potential in a scheme he had promoted briefly in 1936—hiring European noblemen as dance parters for female guests in Casa Mañana. He contacted his longtime press agent, Richard Maney, and Maney, in turn, contacted the Noblemen's Club, an organization of displaced but legitimate royals who had banded together and met monthly in a New York City hotel. Maney offered any gentleman offering proof of noble ancestry seventy-five dollars a week and round trip plane fare to Texas. Six of the titled men, exiled from their home countries during the Bolshevik revolution, accepted a one-month contract. As an additional part of the bargain, Rose gained a genuine countess to serve as official hostess and to make sure that all ladies received a formal introduction to their royal partners.

Once they had arrived in Fort Worth, Rose ensconced his nobles in a specially designed "royal box," outfitted with plush curtains and blazoned with its own royal crest, a gold crown. As an added touch he ordered engraved "invitations" bearing the same crest. These were then distributed to ladies in the audience each evening. The tone of the invitation was kept properly formal:

> If you feel like dancing tonight and your escort doesn't,
> with his permission,
> Billy Rose invites you to dance with one of the following gentlemen:
> Marquis Bruno Pepe Dei Volpicelli
> Baron Georgs Van Der Veer
> Count Nico Veggetti Di Caffa
> Pasha Ilias Toptani
> Count Adam Skarbek
> Count Alexis Pantaleoni
> Ask your nearest Captain. The Countess Helen Massy-Dawson will
> introduce the gentleman to you.[6]

As a promotional gimmick, the importation of titled dance partners was an unqualified success. Rose extended their contract to six weeks, and throughout their stay, the foreign visitors were feted and entertained in the best homes as local society vied for a chance to hobnob with royalty. The noblemen accepted the attention with aplomb, treating the episode as an adventure and a chance to develop friendships and business opportunities. Only two snags threatened the proceedings. One occurred when Rose, seeking to help Mike Romanoff, an out-of-work show business acquaintance, attempted to introduce him as a bogus "prince" into the royal box. The noblemen struck and refused to end the boycott until Rose banished the impostor. The next day Rose staked Romanoff to some cash and a train ticket to Hollywood. Count Veggetti Di Caffa staged a second protest after reading comments by a New York columnist characterizing him as a "gigolo."[7] Although no permanent hard feelings resulted from either incident, at the end of their contract, most of the blue bloods chose to return to New York and the "royal" box was stripped.

A small item in the *Star-Telegram* noted that "Mary Martin, daughter of Mr. and Mrs. Preston Martin of Weatherford, is known in Hollywood as the 'Texas Debutante.' She makes her film debut in Universal's 'Merry Go Round of 1938.'"[8] Ironically, it was Martin's fateful rejection by Billy Rose a year earlier that led her finally to desert her hometown and seriously pursue a show business career. The small item about a girl whose only association with Casa Mañana came through losing an audition demonstrated Fort Worth's continuing fascination with the Frontier Fiesta in general and with Casa Mañana in particular. No incident or event was too minor for the hometown press. Reporters compiled meticulous lists of the more prominent Casa Mañana partygoers for a daily column titled "Frontier Fiesta Visitors." Metro-Goldwyn-Mayer filmed a short subject movie of "It Can't Happen Here," laboring on the theater's revolving stage till dawn for several evenings in order to complete the project. Members of the Casa Mañana ensemble served as cast members. Backstage feuds, romances, broken engagements, wrenched knees, sprained ankles, who was seen with whom at what party, and one appendectomy—all fed locals' seemingly insatiable appetite for news of what was perceived as the "glamorous" lives of Casa Mañana performers. In the show's ninety-three-day run, *Press* and *Star-Telegram* columnists chronicled four weddings, two divorces, and hundreds of gossipy items worthy of Hollywood's chief gossip columnists, Hedda Hopper and Louella Parsons. In the early morning hours of September 4, after Casa Mañana's final show of the evening, Marjorie Groffel and Dominique Childs were finally married in The Little Church on the Sunset Trail. The Fiesta paid for the license, the preacher, and the bridal suite. The romance had survived time, distance, and Billy Rose's lockout of New York dancers.[9]

Even before Casa Mañana's 1937 premiere there were clear signs that Rose's personal life and the problems inherent with managing two widely separated exhibitions were having an adverse effect on his ability to manage effectively. Shortly after the fiesta's opening, James North complained to Amon Carter that Pioneer Palace, overloaded with entertainers, still had no show. Only ten dancers and one substitute were needed, but as many as fifteen remained on the payroll. In Casa Mañana the situation was even worse. Lauretta Jefferson, given the responsibility of rehearsing dancers in several big production numbers, had been furnished choreography for only one routine. When only one week remained before the June 26 opening date, Rose continued to hold most of his production staff in Cleveland, although he found time to call North and complain when his paycheck did not arrive on time.[10]

After the Casa Mañana revue ran long in dress rehearsals and opening performances, the decision was made to cut some numbers, including one called the Devil Dance. With key staff members absent, however, the decision came too late to cancel costumes for the number—they had already been completed at a cost of $7,500. The Fiesta had to absorb the loss while the costumes hung unused for the remainder of the season. The Calgary Brothers, one of the revue's feature acts, became another victim of the time overruns. Rose promised the performers that he would find them work, but two weeks after being cut from the roster, they remained on the payroll, with the fiesta obliged to pay their $3,000 in salary and lost bookings. North blamed Rose's indifference to everything but his own paycheck, saying, "Whenever he throws out an act, it's a saving; he doesn't figure the cost involved in the fact they were unnecessary to start with or he should have figured out the time of the show before. He wants to do all catching and no pitching."[11]

Several weeks after the fiesta's premiere North outlined his growing frustration with Rose in a long memo to Amon Carter. The problems resulting from Rose's frequent absences were only one source of consternation. Fiesta board members additionally discovered that Rose had violated a clause of his contract, one giving the fiesta exclusive rights to all characters, by producing identical finales in Cleveland and Fort Worth. Even with the abuses, North still remained hopeful that he could keep Rose in line and avoid negative press exposure, despite the fact that Casa Mañana, once running a profitable twenty-five percent

Grand Finale, Billy Rose's Cleveland Aquacade—identical to Casa Mañana's "It Can't Happen Here," right down to the miniature battleships (pp. 119-120).

Courtesy Cleveland State University, Cleveland Press Collection.

ahead of the previous season, was only breaking even by July 10. While expressing a personal liking for Rose, he warned Carter that the producer required a firm hand:

> Billy makes some rather amusing demands and cites his contract. I have been fond of the fellow and I don't want to see trouble with him or him leave the show because of the damage such would cause in unfavorable publicity and comment. But I think if he does get too strong or doesn't perform for this show we can bring him quickly around by filing or threatening to file [law] suits.[12]

Meanwhile, as Rose and his Aquacade star Eleanor Holm continued to deny the existence of any relationship other than professional, Holm's husband, bandleader Arthur Jarret, filed for divorce. In his complaint Jarret cited another man, although he stopped short of naming Rose specifically.[13]

At about the same time, new restrictions on liquor sales and renewed accusations of indecency, issues which had their origins in the centennial year, began to resurface. These, together with Rose's desultory attention to fiesta affairs compared with those of a more personal nature, contrived to endanger the welfare and future of Casa Mañana. Billy Rose in 1936 had taken on the seemingly impossible task of mounting from scratch a complete centennial exposition. He had emerged 120 days later as local hero and national celebrity. No request by Rose was too difficult to fulfill. City fathers granted his every whim and blithely looked the other way as he installed the more prurient attractions of the fiesta.

In 1936 because of the importance of federal and tourist dollars, the Texas Liquor Control Board had chosen to overlook laws restricting liquor sales to nothing stronger than beer or wine. By 1937, however, with no centennial to celebrate, the attitude of tolerance had evaporated, and control board agents made frequent surprise tours of fiesta shows, checking for sales of mixed drinks. Not even the passionate outpouring of nationalistic fervor in Casa Mañana's "It Can't Happen Here" could persuade the powerful board to alter its stance. Both press and management decried the negative impact of the new attitude, especially on Casa Mañana's late-night second show.[14] Fiesta profits plummeted by as much as 33 percent.

The ban on the sale of mixed drinks did not, however, prevent Casa Mañana patrons from supplying their own. A package store on the grounds stayed open until midnight each evening to assure that show visitors were amply supplied. Manager of food and drink services for Casa Mañana Tom Daley hired runners who regularly shuttled between dry customers in the cabaret and the store to assure the continual flow of alcoholic refreshment.[15] This contradiction in legalities sometimes produced ironically humorous situations. A Fort Worth city councilman complained to management when, after bringing his own bottle of champagne, he was charged ten dollars for allowing Casa Mañana waiters to uncork and pour for his guests. Drunks continued to cause problems. A Texas A&M cadet slipped into a line of dancers one evening and managed to complete the number, much to the delight of the audience, before being ejected forcibly. A more serious incident occurred as a heckler tossed a liquor bottle at bandleader Paul Whiteman, missed, and struck two female patrons, sending one to the hospital.[16]

To counteract sagging box office sales, Billy Rose announced in August a major overhaul of several shows, including Casa Mañana. Positions were consolidated and staff reduced with some performers, including Harriet Hoctor, Everett Marshall, and the Cabin Kids accepting salary cuts.[17]   James North, fretting in regular memos to Amon Carter about Casa Mañana's sacrifice of comedy to pageantry and culture, had seen it all coming: "More beautiful and higher type than last year, it is not as entertaining and hasn't the repeat value."[18] Receipts for the last week of August in Casa Mañana bore him out, amounting to only $12,947, the lowest of the show's two seasons. Expenses in the same period came to $19,000. There had also been a steady decline in attendance throughout the month—the combined tallies of each evening's two performances averaged only 2,372. For the same period in 1936, average attendance had stood at 4,306.[19]

Rose retrenched with a formula that had served him well in previous shows. He injected several new specialty acts, including pantomimist Joe Jackson, comic jugglers The Three Cossacks, and the dance team of Harrison and Fisher. Casa performers also began late-night rehearsals to revive a crowd pleasing dance number from the Chicago sequence of the 1936 Cavalcade of World's

Fairs Revue. The show-stopping finale featured line after line of furiously step-ping chorus boys and girls linked arm in arm four abreast as they tap danced backward off the revolving stage. Pioneer Palace received a similar face-lift with the addition of dancers Chester Frederick and Art Frank to fill the shoes of Pat Rooney and the addition of comic drunks Fritz and Jean Hubert. Melody Lane, not drawing well in the ill-fated *Jumbo* pavilion, became a free attraction, but "Flirting With Death" closed down completely.

Adding to the fiesta's mounting financial difficulties, the Fort Worth City Council adopted a newly conservative attitude toward some of the more "bur-lesque" aspects of the celebration, a change in moral stance curiously contra-dicting the relatively tolerant attitudes of the preceding centennial year. This new conservatism emerged, evidently, in response to the repeated outcry from local religious groups against indecency in the 1936 Texas Centennial and Frontier Centennial shows. Writing in the *Baptist Standard*, Bud Russell decried the lack of a moral stance from civic leaders, saying,

> In this age of flaming youth, when young girls and boys treat sex as a trivial
> matter, there can be but one end to an evening which includes nude shows,
> hip pocket flasks and automobile rides down dark lanes. Perhaps you are
> content to leave the nude performers to their own judgment, but what of
> your daughter and your son?[20]

The Tarrant County Baptist Association brought the accusations of irre-sponsibility closer to home, opening its annual report on civic righteousness with the words,

> We deplore nudity. We believe that nude exhibitions in our Frontier
> Centennial and the wide publicity given this phase of the show has not
> only seriously affected the morals of the people... but that it has given Fort
> Worth a name throughout the nation that the good people of this city do
> not deserve. We believe that the nude exhibitions and publicity of the
> Frontier Centennial.... has so cheapened the show that it has tremendously
> hurt attendance.[21]

The report named the centennial board directly, accusing its members of fis-cal irresponsibility and ignoring prevailing public sentiment:

This board not only did not heed the appeal of the righteous of our city against indecency, but they used the taxpayers' money...to pay the deficit already accumulated on a show that many of our best citizens not only object to, but refuse to attend.[22]

The protests, largely ignored during the centennial year, centered chiefly on the new show in the Pioneer Palace, Hinda Wassau's "bump" dance, titled "The Evolution of the Strip-Tease." Wassau had taken her place among the first ranks of such popular striptease artists as Ann Corio and Gypsy Rose Lee during the depths of the Depression, a time when burlesque experienced unprecedented growth while traditional, conservative vaudeville steadily declined. She, like Sally Rand, had developed a reputation by holding audiences spellbound with graceful, sensuous dancing, while at the same time allowing them to see only what she wished them to see. Like Rand also, she worked under a blue light and maneuvered her dress as she removed it in such a way that audiences caught only brief glimpses of bare skin until the act's finale. *Variety* termed her "one of three or four in the business who are not offensive," however chorus girls appearing in her act stripped less subtly.[23]

Despite the furor surrounding her act, or more likely because of it, Wassau continued to grind out her striptease several times a night. At first the Council merely adopted an official resolution condemning the act. Wassau, the wife of Billy Rose's Cleveland Aquacade representative, Rube Bernstein, in the meantime sunbathed nude on the roof of the Hotel Texas, seemingly oblivious to the controversy. After she complained about peeping toms, the hotel's accommodating management even rigged up a special shelter to protect her privacy. Later, as city officials adopted a hard line and threatened to stop the act altogether, Wassau became combative, vowing to continue her performances. Told that she would have to don a G-string, Wassau responded with "What's indecent about my act? I work under a dark blue light. Besides, don't I wear gloves?" Billy Rose came to the defense of the dancer, complaining, "How are you going to do the evolution of the strip tease in a fur coat?" Despite his protests, within a few days Wassau "stripped" wearing panties and a bra.[24]

The effects of the crackdown spread even to Casa Mañana. In 1936 Sally Rand had managed to charm city officials into forgetting that her act was performed au naturel; but in the moral climate of 1937, show officials were forced to make additional adjustments in the name of decency. Mary "Stuttering Sam" Dowell, who had herself been the center of much popular notice, suddenly began sporting a tiny gold-fringed skirt over one elaborate, and brief, peacock costume, a move described as "another concession to council's cover up campaign." The *Fort Worth Press*, with a sardonic jab at the "Rover Boys of City Council," claimed that Fiesta management was also shopping to find panties for Spotty, the balancing terrier of Casa Mañana's Seidel and Spotty.[25]

The culminating blow to the financial solvency of Casa Mañana came from a totally unexpected source. On September 10, Mrs. John Marsh, a native of Atlanta, Georgia, better known under her pen name, Margaret Mitchell, sued Billy Rose and the Frontier Fiesta, claiming in her suit that Rose had knowingly and without permission "pirated" her novel, *Gone With the Wind*. Originally published June 30, 1936, the romanticized history of the old South had sold nearly one million copies during its first six months in print and made a reluctant celebrity of its author. Mitchell's lawyers sought an immediate court injunction to impound all scenery, costumes, and music until a complete audit of profits from Casa Mañana could be made.

With the closing date of the show little more than a month away, Rose pretended unconcern for the benefit of reporters. Claiming Mitchell could offer no proof that he had plagiarized the "Gone With the Wind" sequence, he backed his assertions by declaring the coincidental burning of the mansion in both the Casa revue and the novel "a thirty year old theatrical trick." Rose neglected to mention other startling "coincidences." The revue's printed program listed no fewer than eight separate characters from *Gone With the Wind* by name, including its protaganists Scarlett O'Hara and Rhett Butler. In July when Mitchell received word through friends of possible foul play, she had dispatched lawyers to Fort Worth, who concluded, after viewing the Casa Mañana revue, that Mitchell had a good case for plagiarism. Not only were the names of characters identical, but the skit followed the plot line of the novel closely. Scarlett O'Hara entered with the Tarleton twins, flirted with Ashley Wilkes, and left with Rhett Butler when Ashley favored the demure Melanie. In the climax the northern army

Mary "Stuttering Sam" Dowell in peacock costume for "Lost Horizon" sequence of 1937 Casa Mañana.

Courtesy Dallas Public Library.

approached, Tara burned, and Scarlett and Rhett sang "Gone With the Dawn," a tune Rose had intended to call "Gone With the Wind," but Irving Berlin had already registered a song under that title. E. Clyde Whitlock, *Star-Telegram* music critic reported that Everett Marshall often slipped and sang the lyrics as "Gone With the Wind" despite the title change.[26]

An intriguing connection also exists between Rose's choice of literary material and his association with John Hay "Jock" Whitney, the man who had bankrolled *Jumbo* and persuaded Rose to take the centennial job in Fort Worth. Whitney, his cousin C. V. Whitney, and his sister Joan Payson provided the bulk of the funds needed by David O. Selznick to begin Selznick International Pictures in the summer of 1935. Whitney became chairman of the board of Selznick International and continued as president of his own movie production company, Pioneer Pictures. At the insistence of C. V. Whitney, David Selznick took over operation of both Pioneer and Selznick International. Except for the technicality of ownership, Selznick termed them one operation. This arrangement set up a congenial bidding contest between the two producers in the spring and early summer of 1936 for movie rights to *Gone With the Wind* even before the June 30 publication of the novel.[27]

After Margaret Mitchell agreed to allow her publisher, MacMillan, to serve as agent in selling the movie rights, the potentially lucrative arrangements were assigned to Annie Laurie Williams, who sent the novel to Katharine Brown, head of Selznick's New York office. Brown urged Selznick to purchase the rights immediately, but he continued to drag his feet for several days. She then enlisted the aid of Whitney, and when he threatened to acquire the book for Pioneer, Selznick finally authorized Brown to acquire the film rights.[28] That Whitney, Rose's mentor, is also closely linked to so lucrative a property as *Gone With the Wind* suggests that Rose's "theatrical trick" may have been a move calculated to link his own name with the novel's success. Rose's early history as a songwriter had demonstrated his adeptness at grabbing profits and credit from writers and composers while actually doing little of the work himself. In light of this, and his friendship with Whitney, it seems reasonable to presume that Rose followed closely the progress of negotiations with Margaret Mitchell for movie rights to her novel.

Billy Rose may have expected theatrical tradition or the tenuous connection of friendship with the Whitney family to carry weight with Margaret Mitchell, but the author had already spent a traumatic year dealing with plagiarists intent on sharing her success. Rose represented the first major threat to the novel's dramatization rights, and Mitchell had no intention of allowing what she considered the setting of a dangerous precedent.

When Mitchell informed Macmillan of Rose's actions, the publisher at first balked at pursuing legal action, emphasizing that publicity surrounding the Texas show had actually benefitted sales of the novel after stories appeared in several national publications, including *Life*. Mitchell, however, remained adamant. She feared that Macmillan's failure to enter the suit would weaken her case against Rose and expressed concern that failure to punish him could open the door for others. Eventually the publisher agreed to enter the suit on condition that Mitchell would be responsible for any costs involved.[29]

In an awkward attempt at conciliation, Rose countered the charges by inviting Mitchell and her husband, John Marsh, to view the Fiesta as his guests in Fort

The "Gone With the Wind" sequence, 1937.

Courtesy Dalton Hoffman private collection.

Worth. In Rose's version of what happened next, Marsh rebuffed the overture, explaining that his wife shunned publicity. Rose blustered, "If that's so, why did she write the book?" Stephens Mitchell, Margaret Mitchell's brother and one of the lawyers representing her, offered a markedly different version of the incident. When the Marshes refused the offer, Rose swore, claimed he could do whatever he wanted with the novel, and threatened them with the adverse publicity which would attend a prolonged court battle if they did not drop the suit.[30]

Behind the scenes, Rose's attorneys were desperately seeking an extension of the preliminary hearing date, fearing the effects a court ordered injunction might have on show profits. The original hearing, scheduled for September 10, was moved to September 14. But on that date the court refused to grant another postponement and ordered Rose's 5 percent personal cut of the gate profits impounded, although the injunction stopped short of seizing sets and costumes. James F. Pollock, the fiesta's business manager claimed Rose's take of the gross receipts was only 2.5 percent, half the figure estimated by Mitchell's attorneys. However, the earliest date the court would grant fiesta attorneys for presenting counter arguments was September 27.[31]

This refusal to grant any further extensions proved to be the final blow. On September 14, the same day as the hearing, Rose suddenly announced that the original closing date of the Fiesta was being moved up from October 16 to September 26, one day before the final hearing. Reasons stated publicly for the premature closing included the early approach of fall weather and a previous commitment for Paul Whiteman and his band, although it seemed obvious Rose hoped to minimize his personal losses in any unfavorable court ruling. It is also probable that the Frontier Fiesta Board, in light of James North's earlier warnings, decided to divorce itself as much as possible from the entire affair. They did not want to have Fort Worth and the Fiesta connected with any illegal actions by Rose. Several years later *Star-Telegram* reporter Bess Stephenson observed that Rose probably would have been on the way out anyway. After the slot machines, cowboys, Indians, cavalrymen, square dancers, giants, midgets, showgirls, and stripteasers of 1936, a cavalcade of best sellers held about as much excitement as a ballerina at a prize fight. Stephenson noted wryly, "It was all too refined and anticlimactic. The bookish conception at Casa Mañana had left everybody with an empty feeling."[32]

For Rose himself the September 25 date was more a symbolic closing than a true ending. Unwilling to let his golden goose expire without attempts at resuscitation, "Billy Rose's Show of Shows" opened before enthusiastic Fort Worth audiences on November 5, following tryouts in Brownwood. The revue, whose program opened with the modest proclamation, "In the current decade no brighter star has appeared in the world of entertainment than Billy Rose," featured many of the Casa Mañana showgirls and dancers in numbers from several of Rose's previous shows.

There were signs of trouble from the beginning of the tour. Many theaters, built on a much smaller scale than Casa Mañana, could not accommodate the dance numbers, sometimes calling for twenty-four girls in a line. Rose also economized uncomfortably on travel arrangements for performers. The Six Tiny Rosebuds, oversized favorites of the 1936 Fiesta brought in from Cleveland to join the cast, slept two to a berth on the train like everyone else. Rose himself did not suffer through the same inconvenience. Dancers observed him sneaking Eleanor Holm onto the train.

On November 12, following months of denial, Rose announced that he and his Aquacade star would indeed wed. Fanny Brice, in California to appear in a movie, learned of her impending divorce, like the rest of America, from reading newspaper accounts of the scandal.[33] On December 4, after several weeks of playing to half-empty houses, the "Show of Shows" closed abruptly in San Francisco without previous notice to stunned performers. *Press* amusements editor Jack Gordon dubbed it "The Fold of Folds." In January 1938, Rose finally settled out of court with Margaret Mitchell, agreeing to pay $3,000 plus an additional $25,000 if any further attempts at piracy came to light. In April 1938, in a personal letter to Frontier Fiesta Board chairman, Will K. Stripling, Mitchell apologized for involving the organization in her action against Rose and in a further conciliatory gesture, presented Stripling with the copy of *Gone With the Wind* used in the litigation.[34] On this final anticlimactic note, Fort Worth ended forever its professional association with Billy Rose.

"LET'S PLAY FAIR"

The copyright dispute between Billy Rose and Margaret Mitchell worked oddly to the advantage of both Rose and Fort Worth. Mitchell's litigation eventually absolved fiesta officials of blame, and, additionally, provided an excuse to disassociate themselves and the city officially from the controversy swirling around Rose. Only one final act still remained to expurgate the last traces of his dynasty and complete the dissolution. The fiesta board announced its intentions to sell most of the Frontier Fiesta's portable assets at bargain prices beginning on January 29, 1938, and invited the public to the sale. Twenty-five clerks were required to ring up hundreds of purchases made by shoppers who swarmed onto the showgrounds and began carting off spangled hats, plumes, felt Oriental Yogi costumes, and unused bolts of black net and pink tarlatan from the costume shop; miniature horses from "Wake Up and Live"; guns, a banjo, lamp posts, stovepipe hats, posthole diggers, and turnstiles from the Sunset Trail; even seventeen unclad dressmaker dummies fiesta manager James F. Pollock called his Russian army. Most purchases seemed more sentimental than practical, but one fellow offered Pollock $10 for the mountains from "The Last Frontier," claiming he could salvage enough lumber to add a new wing to his dairy barn. A West Texas farmer bought much of Casa Mañana's scenery, evidently for the same purpose, not out of any great appreciation for musical revues and dancing girls. After the sale, much of the former showground was razed, except for the Pioneer Palace.[1]

If Rose cared what Texans or anyone else thought of his personal or business indiscretions, he gave little indication publicly. With the closing of both the

Sun Valley sequence, Casa Mañana, 1939. Stagehands repaired the artificial "ice" with a blow torch. A benevolent hockey team lent skates to dancers when theirs failed to arrive in time for rehearsals to begin.

Courtesy Special Collections, UTA.

Fort Worth and Cleveland entertainments, the flop of "Show of Shows," legal problems, and continuing vilification in the press for his amorous indiscretions, Rose's fumbling explanation did little to rehabilitate his image. Snapped coming out of a Denver hotel arm in arm with Eleanor Holm, he agreed to an interview after the reporter refused to kill the story. Queried about his breakup with Fanny Brice, Rose once again exhibited his flair for social gaffe, declaring, "There is no fun being married to an electric light."[2] The comment set off a national backlash, the tabloid and media scandal of the moment. Walter Winchell condemned the incident during his regular radio broadcast, saying, "Billy Rose may be in the public eye, but Fanny Brice will always be in the public heart."[3]

His reputation as a cad secure, Rose returned to the New York nightclub scene in the fall of 1937 after a two-year absence, intent on the pursuit of a bigger prize—the New York World's Fair. Perhaps not coincidentally, while still embroiled in legal and marital problems, Rose leased the French Casino nightclub. With the help of his Fort Worth production staff, he began finalizing plans to open a scaled-down indoor version of Casa Mañana, complete with a revolving, retractable stage capable of elevating and turning as it moved forward. The only missing pieces were a lagoon and the water curtain. To retain the feel of the outdoors, Rose replaced these lost elements with the Palm Beach Bar, with lounge chairs, private cabanas, and sunlamps for patrons wishing to improve their tans.[4] Meanwhile, despite several rebuffs by world's fair entertainment director John Krimsky, Rose pressed ahead in his campaign to secure one of the lucrative entertainment concessions for the upcoming event. In his next strategy, Rose simply adjusted his sights, taking direct aim at fair President Grover Whalen and the fair's executive committee. At a presentation arranged through a state senator, Rose armed himself with newsreel footage of both the Cleveland and Fort Worth expositions and the MGM two-reeler of the 1936 Casa Mañana. Despite the high-caliber ammunition, Rose still failed to impress fair officials with the need for such a large-scale revue and left once again without a contract offer.[5]

With several weeks still to go before his new nightclub opened, Rose thought of a way to showcase his talents one last time for fair officials. Although construction proceeded on Casa Mañana's posh interior, he had yet to finalize the entertainment lineup for the nightspot. Within two weeks of the rejection by fair officials, Rose and John Murray Anderson had scripted a new revue based around the theme of the search for talent to attract visitors to the world's fair. Titled conspicuously, "Let's Play Fair," the show featured all new musical numbers by Dana Suesse, an original book and lyrics, and production numbers written expressly to attract the notice of Grover Whalen. Rose and Anderson had first successfully used this thematic approach for *Jumbo*, honed and refined the format in the Cleveland Aquacade and Casa Mañana revues of 1936 and 1937, and now proposed to expend the same effort for a nightclub revue. To make it work, Rose began advertising that Casa Mañana's premiere would feature no fewer than fifty Texas dancers and showgirls led by Mary "Stutterin' Sam" Dowell. At the same time he assembled a cast that included many of the same performers and specialty acts given top billing in the original Casa Mañana and Pioneer Palace. The list included Sally Rand, Morton Downey, Tom Patricola, the Stuart Morgan Dancers, Walter Dere Wahl, Sanami and Michi, Harriet Hoctor, Paul Seidel and Spotty, and the Tiny Rosebuds (rechristened the Elsa Maxwell Girls for the occasion). Abe Lyman's orchestra signed to provide the music and even stripper Hinda Wassau appeared, although later Rose had to drop her act when the deputy police commissioner threatened to close the show.[6] To assure the notice of the right people, Rose leaked word of the show's content to the gossip columnists and announced that matinee idol Oscar Shaw would star as Grover Whalen himself.

If Rose hoped the publicity might pique Whalen's curiosity, the strategy worked. Whalen phoned almost immediately to inquire if Rose intended to libel him after the recent rejection by the fair committee. Rose assured Whalen of his honorable intentions and invited Whalen and the other members of the committee to attend the show's premiere as his guest. Whalen took the bait. When Casa Mañana and "Let's Play Fair" opened on January 18, 1938, to an audience of 1,100 invited dignitaries, celebrities, and members of New York society, Whalen arrived early, accompanied by other fair officials, to claim a front table and drink a complimentary magnum of champagne provided by Rose.

The elaborate revue consisted of twenty-two scenes jammed with artists, vaudeville acts, production numbers, and gorgeously, if scantily, clad chorus girls. Another member of Rose's Fort Worth and Cleveland production team, Raoul Pène du Bois, designed both the costumes and the settings, including a scaled-down version of the Shangri-La scene from the Fort Worth Casa Mañana. Du Bois outdid even himself in the all-out effort to impress Whalen. One dress, suspiciously reminiscent of the Symbol of Peace from "It Can't Happen Here," required forty-eight people to manipulate its eighty-five-foot train and contained 500 yards of satin.[7]

Grover Whalen, in an expansive mood after an evening of flattery and too much champagne, suggested that Rose drop by his office to discuss the world's fair. Rose showed up the next day packing $100,000 in cash, a flamboyant gesture intended to convince Whalen that he was no sideshow producer. When he departed, Rose held an exclusive contract from fair officials in exchange for ten percent of the gross.[8]

Casa Mañana, the nightclub that played such an important role in winning the contract, continued to operate until May of 1939. Rose replaced "Let's Play Fair" with a variety format featuring both headliners and vaudeville acts, the same formula he had used so successfully in *Jumbo* and the original Casa Mañana. By the time the club shut its doors permanently in May 1939, Rose had given starts to Betty Hutton, Ethel Waters, Danny Kaye, Vera-Ellen, and a young Van Johnson. In addition, his changing bill of "Streamlined Varieties" featured such greats as Helen Morgan, the Three Stooges, Jack Benny, and Lou Holtz.[9]

In early 1938, as Billy Rose continued to bask in the glow of his dual triumphs in New York City, Fort Worth officials were baffled by what to do next. Rose's digressions from the conventions of polite behavior had angered influential members of the fiesta board, but, at the same time, his drive and audacity had focused national attention on the city.

The question was resoundingly answered when growing public clamor convinced officials that a revival of at least Casa Mañana would find support in the community. But as late as June 1, nothing had been finalized. Originally plans had called for a season opening around July 15, but the necessity of holding local dance auditions and a change in the final awarding of the production contract most likely necessitated the delay.[10] The Chamber of Commerce voted to try and work out an agreement with Fortune Gallo of the San Carlo Opera Company.

To mount the new Casa Mañana Revue, officials eventually reached an agreement with Music Corporation of America, the organization behind the operations of Radio City Music Hall. MCA, under the leadership of producer Lou Wasserman and director Paul Oscard, continued in the established Roseian tradition of packaging big-name bands and nationally known entertainers but rotated the appearance of the featured stars on a fortnightly basis instead of booking acts for the entire season. This strategy marked a significant departure from the Rose era and continued through both the 1938 and 1939 seasons. Other changes in Casa Mañana attested to an almost spartan economizing—a clear move away from the flamboyance of the Rose era, with officials even ordering the draining of the Casa Mañana lagoon. Pioneer Palace, the only other major building remaining from the Frontier Centennial, reopened as a dime-a-dance nightspot. Replacing the monumental scenic dimensions of "Lost Horizon" and "It Can't Happen Here" were uncomplicated banks of rainbow-colored lights placed in the windows of arches onstage. Operating costs dropped to $17,500 a week but led to fears that the cutbacks would alienate theatergoers accustomed to Roseian extravagance. Showgirl Beth Lea recalled her dismay at the new policies in the absence of Rose: "It just wasn't as pretty after that. Billy Rose had the money—he was bankrolled; these people weren't. They [MCA] were just people who came in to make a little money and spend as little as possible." In spite of such newfound austerity, by opening day, July 29, promoters announced a sell out of all 4,000 seats.[11]

During the first two weeks of the run, orchestra leader Wayne King anchored the main bandstand providing accompaniment for show numbers as well as late-night music for dancing. On August 12, Jan Garber's band took over for the remainder of the season. Assisting in the second bandstand for the entire run was a group of local musicians under the baton of Ed Lally, adding what *Variety* called a "Texas touch" to the show. Headlining entertainers included tenor Morton Downey, dancer Edna Sedgwick, and ventriloquist Edgar Bergen, who appeared for two performances only. Also scheduled were comedians George Burns and Gracie Allen, who canceled their engagement at the last moment.[12] Avoiding the thematic approach adopted by Rose and his team, Wasserman and Oscard focused instead on lavish production numbers and topnotch stars to provide the needed framework.

The seven variety acts completing the bill offered something for every taste in the long-established vaudeville tradition—the Three Nonchalants, a knock-about comedy trio; the Peggy Taylor Trio, yet another adagio acrobatic team; comedian Horton Spurr, "The Man Who Bounces," in a slow-motion pantomime of the world's worst golfer; Monroe and Grant, trampoline comedians; Serge Flash, "juggler extraordinary"; and Walter Nillson, cycle comedian. In between

these the forty Casa Mañana dancers and twelve statuesque showgirls, by now
seasoned show business veterans themselves, appeared in lavish production
numbers choreographed by Lauretta "Jeffie" Jefferson, Robert Alton's assistant
throughout the two-year run of the Frontier Centennial and Fiesta. Assisting her
was Alexander Oumansky, another centennial holdover. The quality of the
dancing was exceptional; the costumes, however, were rented.[13]

On July 29 William Monnig officially opened the 1938 Casa Mañana with
a sardonic allusion to previous controversies. "I'm ex-councilman Monnig," he
quipped. "If I hadn't had my picture made with Sally Rand once, I'd still be a
councilman."[14] Then, in tradition established during the 1936 centennial year,

Showgirls with Morton Downey,
one of the 1938 headliners.

Courtesy Special Collections, UTA.

the giant stage revolved once more as Wayne King's band swung into "The Night Is Young and You're So Beautiful." The audience saw forty chorus girls adorned in cellophane costumes and capes, which they "rippled" to simulate water flowing from a fountain. The scene reminded one reviewer enough of the Roseian preoccupation with bare flesh to comment, "When they break from the formation, they fill the stage with shimmering fringe, shapely curves and not much else. This is the number that might give the girls pneumonia if a cold snap blew in."[15]

The other numbers in Casa Mañana's first venture under new management spotlighted current trends in music and dance. The night's second scene, a "hot rhumba," featured headliner Edna Sedgwick performing a Spanish fandango backed by the chorus in ruffled silver taffeta skirts. The dancing ensemble returned after intermission costumed in "seductive purple satin" for the third big number of the evening, "American Bolero." Edna Sedgwick, resplendent in a gold-sequined evening gown, danced through a medley of popular hits including Ravel's "Bolero," "Night and Day," and "Deep Purple." To close out the evening, the fifty-two-member ensemble, both featured bands, and Morton Downey combined in a red-white-and-blue rendition of "The Eyes of Texas Are Upon You." Attendance was estimated at 23,000 for the first week and gross receipts of $17,900 heartened local businessmen underwriting the season. Morton Downey had his contract extended an extra two weeks, and producers discussed extending the planned four-week season an extra two weeks past Labor Day.[16]

The second fortnight of the 1938 season saw an all-new bill of production numbers, featured performers, and variety bill, except for Morton Downey. The new lineup of variety acts featured top-billed Hal Silver, tightwire comedian; comic team Dare and Yates; Ames and Arno, who billed themselves as "Two Social Errors" and burlesqued the adagio dance teams in vogue all through the decade; and The Olympics, "daredevil roller skaters." Completing the bill were tap dancer Sunny O'Day, swing singer Patricia Norman, and hoop-rolling comedians Jack Gregory and Company. Four brand new production numbers made their debut including one that featured the cast dressed in Robin Hood and Maid Marian costumes, capitalizing on the popularity of screen idol Errol Flynn's latest movie swashbuckler, *The Adventures of Robin Hood*. In another sequence the dancing ensemble and showgirls paraded behind large ostrich fans, trading on the Sally Rand mystique. *Variety* reported, "[The] show pleases customers better than Casa of 1937, even though not quite so spectacular. It makes up in talent what it lacks in that respect." As business continued to build, MCA sent its top executive, J. C. Stein, to view the show with an eye to expanding the corporation's management interests into the outdoor theater market.[17]

The cabaret theater welcomed the largest audience in its three-year history on August 24 when a sizable portion of the Fort Worth theatergoers turned out for ventriloquist Edgar Bergen and his wooden sidekicks, Charlie McCarthy and Mortimer Snerd. Three days later, on August 27, the season ended on a positive

Amon G. Carter with ventriloquist Edgar Bergen and Bergen's wooden sidekick, Charlie McCarthy.

Courtesy Special Collections, UTA.

note when backers estimated that 90,000 paid admissions had passed through the turnstiles during the abbreviated season. Despite the time lost through the tentativeness of planners and the necessity of spending $22,000 to refurbish the theater and properties, gross receipts still tallied up to $86,000 with an estimated $6,800 net profit. Although the show was extended only two days past its original planned closing date of August 25, the profit calculations encouraged producer Lou Wasserman to recommend an expanded sixty-eight-day season for 1939. Confidence ran so high that Casa Mañana's permanence seemed assured beyond any doubt.[18]

On the surface, the 1939 season did little to dispel this notion. Under the aegis of New York talent moguls the William Morris Agency and executive producer Lou Wolfson, Casa Mañana opened its fourth season on July 21 with a cotillion scene of white-gowned debutantes waltzing to the romantic strains of "The Night Is Young and You're So Beautiful." The parade of talent through the summer was impressive: Kenny Baker, a regular on Jack Benny's weekly radio program; comedienne Martha Raye, who claimed to have been born in a trunk backstage; Bob Burns, the "Arkansas Traveler"; Ziegfeld legend Eddie Cantor; and a young Ray Bolger, veteran of the Ziegfeld Follies and fresh from completion of his role as the Scarecrow in a new movie, *The Wizard of Oz*. Frances Langford, popular featured singer of the Texaco Star Theater, arrived in Fort Worth accompanied by movie-star husband Jon Hall, who had made his mark in the 1937 melodrama, *The Hurricane*. Also appearing were local favorite Everett West, popular former member of the California Varsity Eight; singer Tony Martin; the Elite Trio; ice skaters Adele Inge and Frenchie Herbert; dance team DeAngelo and Porter; and Bob Williams and his trained dog, Red Dust. The bands of Russ Morgan, Abe Lyman, and Ray Noble were all featured. By the end of the show's first two weeks, attendance figures were even better than for the same period in 1938 with audiences still building and $38,000 in gross earnings.[19]

The week-long engagement of comedian Eddie Cantor, while marking one of the high points of the 1939 season, also became a harbinger of rapidly converging events that would lead to the amphitheater's permanent closure. Cantor, a show business veteran who had come up through the ranks of vaudeville to

Ray Bolger rehearsing

Courtesy Special Collections, UTA.

earn feature billing in the Ziegfeld Follies, movies, and legitimate theater, had first come to Fort Worth in Gus Edwards' "Kid Cabaret," booked into the old Majestic Theater in 1912. For his Casa Mañana engagement Cantor opted for a curly blonde wig, gingham dress, and white apron to warble "On the Good Ship Lollipop," in a parody of child star Shirley Temple. In other segments he donned blackface, a Cantor trademark from his vaudeville days, and interspersed popular songs with short monologues. Cantor, a tireless critic of Adolf Hitler, used his appearance in Fort Worth as a platform to warn of the growing threat to world peace presented by the German dictator's policies of aggression and racial persecution. He interjected a somber note into his performance by including in his numbers one entitled, "The Dogs of War Are Growling."

Once again, in the by-now-familiar formula, specialty acts and several elaborate production numbers were interspersed throughout the show. One scene, set in the ski resort of Sun Valley, included an elaborate ice-skating sequence—the

Publisher Amon Carter, Sr., and Ziegfeld Follies star Eddie Cantor pose with teenage performer of 1939 Casa Mañana Virginia Joyce.

Courtesy the private collection of Mrs. Virginia Joyce Cox.

"ice" was artificial and could be repaired with a blow torch. Skates for the dancers did not show up in time for the beginning of rehearsals. To fill in, more skates had to be found. The only available ones, finally located in Oklahoma, belonged to the members of an all-male ice hockey team and were several sizes too big. Girls in the sequence carried on anyway, stuffing the toes of the borrowed skates with paper. Finally, only three days before the scheduled opening, the more dainty figure skates arrived.[20] Another scene was composed entirely of the most popular song and dance numbers from Casa Mañana's first three seasons. It was a moment of supreme nostalgia for many theater regulars, made unwittingly more poignant by the fact that the 1939 season was destined to be the last for the outdoor cabaret.

On Friday, September 1, Germany invaded Poland. Two days later, on September 3, one day before the end of the Casa Mañana season, Britain and France jointly declared war in retaliation. That same evening, shortly before 8:00 P.M., pre-show dancing on the Casa Mañana stage was halted so that theater patrons and citizens across the nation could listen to a nationally broad-cast message from President Franklin Roosevelt that ended with his somber promise, "As long as it remains within my power to prevent, there will be no blackout of peace in the United States."[21] Following the address, the audience stood automatically for the playing of the "Star-Spangled Banner," but the singing that usually accompanied its playing was noticeably subdued. Although the show resumed with no more interruptions, the festive mood of the partygoers had evaporated. Breaking news on September 4 reporting the sinking of the *Athenia*, whose passenger list included many Americans, marred the revue's final night. Further presaging the dark events that would contribute to the demise, newspapers carried stark photographs of fleeing refugees and German warplanes sweeping relentlessly over Poland.[22]

The growing recognition of the inevitability of war caused a clear change in public sentiment toward Casa Mañana and erased the final vestiges of centennial ebullience. Through 1940 and 1941 supporters mounted several unsuccessful campaigns to reopen Casa Mañana, but ironically, the huge amphitheater had become a victim of its own success. Constructed largely of plywood, literally thrown together in a matter of months, it had never been intended as permanent and after four seasons was falling down. No one could have foreseen its immense popularity or the stimulating effect on the economy and spirits of Depression-weary Fort Worth. A bond proposal seeking $225,000 to reconstruct the theater as a permanent structure failed to gather the necessary support despite a *Star-Telegram* editorial that sternly warned, "if the structure is not made permanent now the cost of so making it later will be prohibitive due to rapid deterioration and a huge investment will have been lost." A coalition made up of thirty-four Baptist, Methodist, and Presbyterian churches elected Reverend C. E. Matthews chairman and began circulating petitions opposing the proposition. The group claimed a tax increase would result, although it seems equally likely that accusations of indecency played a prominent role in the opposition to the theater's continued operation. More importantly, detractors questioned the wisdom of tying up valuable construction materials in an entertainment facility that had lost $1,100,000 for its investors when these same materials were already earmarked for defense and denied to contractors for new home construction.[23]

The issue never reached the voters. With the war in Europe escalating steadily, on November 5, 1941, the city council postponed the question indefinitely, effectively killing the proposition. Then on December 7 the United States officially entered World War II with the bombing of Pearl Harbor, and all hopes of saving Casa Mañana went down with the American battleship fleet. The following year, on May 11, 1942, demolition began on the massive structure once touted as the showpiece of the nation. Hundreds of Fort Worthians streamed by the theater in a final tribute as workmen began the dismantling process. The crowds increased steadily until the police department had to station a special officer nearby to prevent souvenir hunters and sentimental onlookers from interfering with the orderly destruction of the landmark. A workman ripping out the floor of the revolving stage came across a faded pair of dancing shoes, a final reminder of past glories. A former chorus girl pleaded with the officer to allow her one last glimpse of the old dressing rooms. The policeman finally relented. A few minutes later the young woman returned, softly weeping into her handkerchief. Jack Gordon of the *Fort Worth Press* noted the theater's passing with

sadness: "Salvagers may tear away the rottened planks of Casa Mañana, but they can't take away the town's memories." Bess Stephenson, writing the official epitaph for Amon Carter's *Star-Telegram*, noted inconsistencies in the operations of the theater which contributed to its problems. While characterizing the final season of 1939 as "a valiant and costly effort to crowd the place with big names and make [Casa Mañana] an endearing haven again," she also observed that "some of the biggest and costliest names flopped where unknowns had won glory in 1936."[24] Despite this, Stephenson's parting sentiments stand as a poetically bittersweet eulogy to the theater's power over the community. Recalling 1936 as the theater's halcyon year, she wrote,

Pioneer Palace and the Casa Mañana stage machinery lie derelict after the theater's destruction in the 1940s.

Courtesy Special Collections, UTA.

That was a year of splendor and romance and incredible miracles. It was a year of dazzling beauty and warm-hearted gaiety and wholly magnificent gestures. It was a year of extravagance, too, and of picturesque memorable nonsense . . . now with three seasons of neglect Casa Mañana is a forlorn skeleton. Weather has opened gaps in the floor and washed way the paint that gave the world a new color—Casa Mañana blue. In the wings are blurred and indistinct reminders of romance. The old love has been dead a long time. Next week it will be buried.[25]

When the professional destroyers completed their work ten weeks later, only the huge steel skeleton of the revolving stage remained as a rusting, bleak reminder of what had truly been the Casa Mañana era.[26]

EPILOGUE

If Casa Mañana was gone, its impact on Fort Worth remained. As American fighting men returned home at war's end in 1945, the tide of renewed optimism sweeping across the country brought a fresh surge of interest in reviving the bond issue to resurrect the old theater. A new proposal brought before the city council, while not specifically naming Casa Mañana, called for a principal sum of $500,000 for the purpose of "constructing, building and equipping a recreation center and amphitheater for said city and acquiring the necessary land therefor."[1] The issue came before the voters on October 2, 1945, and passed, but the bonds remained unissued for lack of a viable plan. As Fort Worth concentrated on postwar municipal problems, the unsold entertainment bonds were gradually forgotten.

The transition from war to peace also brought momentous changes in the professional theater. The variety show format popularized by Billy Rose and other major producers, which had dominated Broadway for decades, was fading as the postwar era ushered in the heyday of the musical. The trend had begun as early as 1943 when the success of Rodgers and Hammerstein's *Oklahoma!* revived the dreams of producers, writers, and investors hoping for similar glory and profits. The public also caught the fever and eagerly snapped up tickets for each new musical that Broadway churned out. *South Pacific* in 1949 had an advance ticket sale of $300,000, a record for its time period. The great successes of postwar years merely served to underscore the high standards being achieved by musicals. Between 1945 and 1951, several unprecedented hits, including *Annie Get Your Gun*, *Kiss Me Kate*, and *The King and I*, arrived on Broadway, destined to become staples of the musical theater for decades. The tide surged on unbroken through the late 1950s with such remarkable smash hits as *West Side Story*, *The Sound of Music*, *Camelot*, and *My Fair Lady*.[2]

In the years following World War II, a second important movement caught the imagination of the theater-going public. The idea of musical theater-in-the-round, served up in a circus tent and transplanted to a natural, outdoor setting was generally credited to St. John Terrell, a former carnival fire-eater and the voice of radio's Jack Armstrong. As an entertainment coordinator for the USO during World War II, Terrell had discovered that many troops at remote bases were deprived of entertainment for lack of a stage. Remembering his circus days, Terrell suggested digging out a saucer of earth and then erecting a tent. The USO rejected the idea, but following the war, Terrell used his own back pay, cashed in war bonds, and borrowed additional money to finance his idea of musicals in a tent.[3]

Evidently the public agreed with Terrell's concepts, despite the initial scoffing of many Broadway insiders and critics. There was only one musical tent in 1949. But by 1958, twenty-seven canvas tops had opened with six more scheduled to begin operation that same summer. In the ten seasons from 1949 to 1958, thirteen million Americans saw well-known musicals and operettas staged in the round for an estimated box office profit of $25,000,000. In 1958 it was estimated that three million Americans would queue up outside the tents.[4]

The lure of the "music circus" was irresistible for the grass-roots theatergoer. Even if theater seats were nothing more than folding chairs and floors mere dirt covered with straw, no patron was ever farther from the stage than fifteen or sixteen rows. Comfortable summer wear of slacks, shorts, or sport clothes was not considered out of place. Another extremely attractive feature was the price. For as little as 90 cents, an individual could have a taste of Broadway practically in his own backyard. An entire family could attend for what it would cost to purchase one orchestra seat in a New York City theater.[5]

The idea of erecting a permanent theater-in-the-round in Fort Worth grew out of a newspaper article in the local press in 1957. The feature centered on the geodesic dome, a revolutionary design pioneered by inventor-philosopher R. Buckminster Fuller and Kaiser Aluminum. Melvin Dacus, general manager of the Fort Worth Opera Association, clipped the article and sent it to oilman and opera board Chairman James Snowden. Snowden liked the concept well enough to obtain preliminary construction and materials estimates from Kaiser. There remained however the problem of working capital. Armed with the feasibility studies done by Kaiser, Snowden drafted a proposal whereby the city would build the amphitheater-recreation center originally authorized by the voters twelve years earlier. But instead of an outdoor cabaret, the new structure would incorporate two aluminum geodesic domes to create a sumptuous, trend-setting indoor playhouse and exhibition arena. An independent non-profit organization, Casa Mañana Productions, Inc., would lease the arena from the city for the annual fee of $25,000 and handle its management.[6]

The Downtown Fort Worth Association, the Junior Chamber of Commerce, and the Hotel Owners Association strenuously opposed the idea, fearing that such a center would disrupt ongoing plans for a $25,000,000 renovation of the downtown area that included a proposed convention center. The city council agreed with Snowden. On January 17, 1958, by unanimous vote, the council approved plans for construction of the Casa Mañana Center. Architects recommended abandoning as too costly the original two-dome plan and its chief feature, a proscenium-style amphitheater. Instead, planners opted for a more economical single-dome theater-in-the-round. Construction architect A. George King projected that costs would run considerably more than the $500,000 originally approved by voters even with the design changes.

The choice of a site seemed logical. What better location for the rebirth of an old idea than the home of its namesake, the original Casa Mañana?[7] Construction on the new Casa began in March of 1958, and work progressed rapidly toward an opening projected for late June. City newspapers daily reported the progress of the sixty-six-foot-high dome as workers assembled its 575 diamond-shaped aluminum panels and then raised them to final position by a giant crane. As the aluminum dome steadily took shape, other workers began dismantling the steel skeleton of the old Casa Mañana stage, hauling away the remains to be sold as scrap. It had lain abandoned since 1942, a final ironic reminder of the glittering amphitheater that had once graced the site.

The director chosen to inaugurate the premiere season of the new Casa Mañana was thirty-five-year-old Michael Pollock, artistic director of the New York City Opera Company. Others named to the production staff included musical director William Baer; choreographer Joann Mann; set designer Hal Shafer; and costume designer Evelyn Norton Anderson.

On July 5, 1958, the reborn Casa Mañana welcomed patrons in a scene strongly reminiscent of another premiere on almost the same spot some twenty-two years earlier. Dressed in white dinner jackets and glittering evening gowns, 1,800 first-nighters gamely slogged their way into the new theater, after thunderstorms turned the unpaved parking lot into a sea of mud. Even the discovery of several leaks in the aluminum dome did little to dampen crowd spirits. The invitation-only audience included many of Fort Worth's most prominent citizens, several show business personalities, and a group of former showgirls and dancers from the 1936 Casa Mañana.

The real star of the evening, however, was the theater. *Life* magazine, which had served as witness to the splendors of the former Casa, once again sent photographers to record the premiere. Jack Gordon of the *Press*, in an obvious reference to the theme of the 1936 Casa Mañana Revue, recalled wistfully, "the night is no longer so young for some but the 'lady' is beautiful. She is a handsome reincarnation of the original."[8]

During its first season and for the next several years, Casa Mañana achieved an amazing level of success for an untried operation at a time when other theaters, older and more established, lost substantial amounts of money. Early criticism of staging techniques as amateurish and more suited to conventional theater gave way to praise for the theater's boldness in experimenting with different techniques.

The performers gracing the round stage of Casa Mañana in the years following its premiere, many of them bright unknowns, served as further compensation for the theater's inherent sound and staging deficits. Actors such as Mace Barrett, Nolan Van Way, and Jack Harrold, if not "name" stars in the theater world, found their own celebrity among Fort Worth theatergoers via Casa Mañana, much as the young performers of the 1930s had done. A young unknown soprano named

Beverly Sills starring in Franz Lehar's venerable operetta, *The Merry Widow*, provided the highlight of the 1958 premiere season. Another high point came with the return of the legendary Sally Rand. First in 1968 and again in 1974, she reprised the acclaimed ballet divertissement.

In its second incarnation Casa Mañana grew steadily toward its own distinct identity and moved away from early attempts to recapture the splendors of its acclaimed predecessor. The theater eventually attained respect for its own strong, individual identity and in the process became a community tradition in its own right, providing a variety of quality entertainment offerings for the increasingly sophisticated theater-going public. Nevertheless, with the expansion and diversification of the community, the continued existence of a theater bearing the name Casa Mañana served as clear testimony to the power and mystique of the original, long-vanished theater as a potent icon in the heritage of Fort Worth.

Notes · · · · · · · · · · ·

· · · · · · Introduction · · · · · ·

[1] Complex engineering allowed the stage superstructure to slide either forward or backward on underwater tracks while revolving a full 360 degrees.

[2] *Variety*, 15 April 1936, 63.

[3] *Fort Worth Star-Telegram*, 4 March 1954, 1-2.

[4] *Star-Telegram*, 28 July 1986 (eve.), 6C.

· · · · · · Chapter One · · · · · ·

[1] Casa Mañana advertising brochure, Box 17, Folder 10, Amon Carter Collection, Amon Carter Museum of Art, Fort Worth, Texas; *Fort Worth Star-Telegram*, 12 July 1936, 6.

[2] *New York American*, 21 July 1936. Part of a composite ad appearing in the *Fort Worth Star-Telegram*, 9 August 1936, 3.

[3] Kenneth B. Ragsdale, *The Year America Discovered Texas* (College Station: Texas A&M Press, 1987), 8-18.

[4] Pierre Vidal-Naquet, ed., *Harper Atlas of World History* (New York: Harper and Row, 1987), 264.

[5] Letter from Cullen F. Thomas to Amon G. Carter, 5 January 1934, Box 39, Folder 13, Carter Collection.

[6] Ragsdale, 32-35.

[7] Letter from Lowry Martin, vice-president, Texas Centennial Committee to all members of the Centennial Advisory Board, 26 July 1934, Box 39, Folder 13, Carter Collection.

[8] Letter from James M. North to S. H. McCarty, 1 June 1934, Box 39, Folder 13, Carter Collection.

[9] Minutes of the Texas Centennial Committee, 16 July 1934, Box 39, Folder 13, Carter Collection.

[10] Minutes of the executive committee, Texas Centennial Committee, 6 September 1934, Box 39, Folder 13, Carter Collection.

[11] Minutes of the executive committee, Texas Centennial Committee, 21 September 1934, Box 39, Folder 13, Carter Collection; *Time*, 8 June 1936, 10-11; *Star-Telegram*, 11 February 1936, 1.

[12] Maurice Zolotow, *Billy Rose of Broadway*, (unpublished manuscript), File MWEZ+nc 25518, Billy Rose Theatre Collection, New York Public Library, 298.

[13] Minutes, Fort Worth City Council, 23 October 1935.

[14] Letter from Amon G. Carter to Fritz Lanham, 12 July 1935, Box 39, Folder 13, Carter Collection. For a detailed analysis of the allocation of city/federal monies to the Fort Worth centennial and other federal projects, see Lois Gray, *History of the Fort Worth Frontier Centennial* (unpublished master's thesis, Texas Christian University), 1938.

[15] *Dallas Morning News*, 21 July 1935, 1, 4.

[16] *Dallas Morning News*, 21 July 1935, 1, 4. The contested grant to Fort Worth came from state centennial funds. Only $550,000 had been set aside from state coffers for grants to cities, but $5 million in requests had been received by the centennial Commission of Control.

[17] Gray, 47-49, 52; *Star-Telegram*, 28 August 1935, 1.

[18] William E. Jary, Jr., ed., *Camp Bowie Fort Worth, 1917-1918* (Fort Worth: B. B. Maxfield Foundation, 1975), 4-5, 8-9.

[19] Gray, 30, 43, 58-59. The Stock Yards Company filed a court injunction against the city seeking to prevent removal of any part of the centennial grounds to another location. The effect of the order was to prevent the disbursement of federal money to the city. As a result, the city had to call an additional bond election for January 1936 to compensate for the anticipated shortfall in funds. The city council based its decision to divide the centennial on the need to leave the livestock exhibits in an existing site with adequate pens and barns close by the stockyards. Stockmen later labeled the 1936 centennial livestock exhibition a failure because most visitors chose to attend amusement exhibits built on the Van Zandt location.

[20] Gray, 49.

[21] K. M. Van Zandt, *Force Without Fanfare: The Autobiography of K. M. Van Zandt*, Sandra Myres, ed. (Fort Worth: Texas Christian University, 1968), 111-23, 144-45. Jerry Flemmons, *Amon: The Life of Amon Carter, Sr. of Texas* (Austin: Jenkins Publishing, 1978), 300; Gray, 49.

[22] *Star-Telegram*, 28 January 1936, 1; 29 January 1936, 1; 11 February 1936, 1. In September 1935, a bond issue approved $687,500 to finance the proposed Fort Worth Centennial Exposition. An additional $250,000 was approved by voters in January 1936. Board chairman William Monnig was in favor of rescinding all contracts for the building of the Will Rogers Memorial Coliseum, Auditorium, and Tower. Other city council members persuaded him that this would unfairly jeopardize the entire Fort Worth Centennial celebration.

[23] Letter from James M. North to Tracy-Locke-Dawson, Inc., 24 September 1934, Box 39, Folder 13, Carter Collection.

[24] Letter from Cullen F. Thomas to Amon G. Carter, 5 January 1934, Box 39, Folder 13, Carter Collection.

[25] Letter from Amon Carter to Walter Holbrook, 26 February, 1936, Box 17, Folder 10, Amon Carter Collection.

[26] *Star-Telegram*, 5 June 1936, 1-2.

· · · · · · CHAPTER TWO · · · · · ·

[1] Alva Johnston, "Colonel Carter of Cartersville," *Saturday Evening Post*, 26 November 1938, 8.

[2] *Dallas Morning News*, 30 April 1939, special picture section, 1.

[3] *Dallas Morning News*, 24 June 1955, 1.

[4] Buckley B. Paddock, ed., *A History of Texas: Fort Worth and the Texas Northwest Edition*, vol. 2, (Chicago: Lewis Publishing, 1922), 600; Julia Kathryn Garrett, *Fort Worth: A Frontier Triumph*, (Austin: Encino, 1972; Fort Worth: TCU Press, 1996) 107-108, 142-143, 172-173.

[5] Paddock, 605.

[6] *Fort Worth Democrat*, 6 November 1875, 1.

[7] "Texas Facts and Fancies," *Austin Weekly Democratic Statesman*, 16 November 1876, 3.

[8] Based on U. S. Geological Survey Map for Tarrant County, 1902, Tarrant Collection, Fort Worth Public Library; S. G. Reed, *A History of the Texas Railroads*, (Houston: St. Clair, 1944), 364, 520-542; *Fort Worth In Story and Picture*,(n.p., n.d.), Women's Division Scrapbook, 1936, Tarrant Collection, Fort Worth Public Library.

[9] Flemmons, 134-138.

[10] Telephone interview with Mrs. Ruth Carter Stevenson, daughter of Amon G. Carter, Sr., November 1997.

[11] Robert H. Talbert, *Cowtown Metropolis: Case Study of a City's Growth and Structure* (Fort Worth: Leo Potishman Foundation, Texas Christian Univ., 1956), 16; Flemmons, 228-234.

[12] Flemmons, 358; *Star-Telegram*, 24 June 1955. Robert J. Serling, *Eagle: The Story of American Airlines* (New York: St. Martin's, 1985), 1-16.

[13] Johnston, 8.

[14] *Federal Writers Project for Fort Worth and Tarrant County*, Fort Worth Public Library, 15745.

[15] Darwin Payne, *Big D: Triumphs and Troubles of an American Supercity in the 20th Century* (Dallas: Three Forks Press, 1994), 208.

[16] Rufus Le Maire (obituary), *Star-Telegram*, 4 December 1950, 1, 4.

[17] Billy Rose, *Wine, Women and Words* (New York: Simon and Schuster, 1948), 15.

[18] Zolotow, 6-12, 68. In February-March 1947 a four-part article written by Zolotow about Rose's career appeared in *Colliers Magazine*. However, there are major differences in the unpublished manuscript and the articles written for *Colliers*. Zolotow claimed to have interviewed over 200 persons including Rose himself and Brice, as well as other actors, musicians, relatives, press agents, producers, writers, and composers who had known or worked with Rose.

[19] Polly Rose Gottlieb, *The Nine Lives of Billy Rose* (New York: Crown, 1968), 58-59; Zolotow, 69-70.

[20] David A. Jasen, *Tin Pan Alley* (New York: Donald I. Fine, 1988), xv-xxi.

[21] Stephen Nelson, *Only a Paper Moon: The Theatre of Billy Rose* (Ann Arbor, Michigan: UMI Research Press, 1987), 3-7.

[22] Nelson, 8-9; Gottlieb, 78-79; Rose, 11.

[23] Nelson, 9, 11-12.

[24] Nelson, 22-28; Zolotow, 229-242.

[25] Quoted by Billy Rose in "Pitching Horseshoes," *New York Daily News*, 8 September 1947 (page unknown); Earl Conrad, *Billy Rose: Manhattan Primitive* (New York: World, 1968), 77-78.

[26] Nelson, 29.

[27] "Grand National," *Time*, 27 March 1933, 20-21.

[28] Gerald Bordman, *The Oxford Companion to American Theatre*, 2nd ed. (New York: Oxford University Press, 1992), 344.

[29] Ben Hecht and Charles MacArthur, *Billy Rose's Jumbo*, music and lyrics by Richard Rodgers and Lorenz Hart, 1935.

[30] Conrad, 105.

[31] Zolotow, 296.

[32] Zolotow, quote attributed to Billy Rose, 297; Rose, 75.

[33] Telegram from Amon Carter to Jock Whitney, 4 March 1936, Box 17, Folder 10, Carter Collection.

[34] *Star-Telegram*, 9 March 1936, 1; 10 March 1936, 1.

[35] Zolotow, quote attributed to Rose, 302-303.

[36] Zolotow, 302.

[37] Zolotow, 303-304.

[38] Zolotow, 304-305.

[39] *Star-Telegram*, 9 March 1936 (eve.), 1.

[40] *Star-Telegram*, 10 March 1936, 1; Zolotow, 305. (None of the quotes in this chapter appeared in the *Colliers* article except for the telegram purportedly sent by Anderson to Rose.)

· · · · · · CHAPTER THREE · · · · · ·

[1] *Fort Worth Press*, 9 July 1936, 7.

[2] *Star-Telegram*, 10 March 1936, 1

[3] Interview with William E. Jary, Fort Worth, October 1985.

[4] *Press*, 9 March 1936, 1.

[5] *Star-Telegram*, 10 April 1936, 1; 11 June 1936, sec. 2, 1; *Press*, 10 April 1936, 14; 6 May 1936, 11.

[6] *Press*, 21 April 1936, 1; *Star-Telegram*, 5 July 1936, society sec., 9.

[7] *Star-Telegram*, 10 March 1936, 1.

[8] *Press*, 9 March 1936, 1.

[9] *Press*, 21 April 1936, 1.

[10] Ibid.

[11] *Variety*, 11 March 1936, 1, 38.

[12] Memo from Billy Rose to Amon Carter, 4 April 1936; memo from Amon Carter to James Record, 8 April 1936, Box 17, Folder 10, Carter Collection.

[13] *Press*, 19 March 1936, 8; *Star-Telegram*, 10 March 1936, 1.

[14] *Billboard*, 14 March 1936, 5; *Variety*, 11 March 1936, 38; Brown's comments were included in an earlier press release furnished to local reporters and quoted in the *Star-Telegram*, 9 March 1936, 4.

[15] Letter from Arthur L. Kramer to William Monnig 19 March 1936; letter from William Monnig to Arthur L. Kramer (n.d.), Box 17, Folder 10, Carter Collection.

[16] Cecilia Ager, "Rose's Main Entrance Gag for Fort Worth to Buck Dallas' Centennial," *Variety*, 15 April 1936, 63.

[17] *Star-Telegram*, 12 May 1936, 12; 13 May 1936 (eve.), 2; 2 July 1936 (eve.), 8.

[18] *Star-Telegram*, 3 June 1936, sec. 2, 1; 9 June 1936, 24; 27 July 1936, 5; *Time*, 8 June 1936, 13 (Joe Peanuts and the Gigolo Band failed to appear—Rose eventually replaced them with another skin show.)

[19] *New York Herald-Tribune*, quoted in *Star-Telegram*, 10 April 1936, 8.

[20] *Star-Telegram*, 7 May 1936, 3; *Press*, 6 May 1936, 1.

[21] *Press*, 1 April 1936, 1.

[22] Official Program, Casa Mañana, 1936; Robert Randol, *Star-Telegram*, 7 July 1936 (eve.), 14.

[23] Taken from various accounts including Casa Mañana program; *Star-Telegram*, 12 April 1936, 1; 14 April 1936, 1; 17 April 1936 (eve.), 1, 4; *Press*, 1 April 1936, 9; 14 April 1936, 1.

[24] *Press*, 1 June 1936, 1, 5.

[25] *Press*, 14 July 1936, 6.

[26] *Press*, 14 July 1936, 1.

[27] Conrad, 105-06.

[28] John Murray Anderson, *Out Without My Rubbers* (New York: Library, 1954), 145-46; Conrad, 125-26.

[29] *Star-Telegram*, 8 June 1936 (eve.), 1, 4.

[30] *Press*, 1 June 1936; 8; Official Program, Casa Mañana, 1936.

[31] *Press*, 17 July 1936, 1; *Star-Telegram*, 23 July 1936 (eve.), 5.

[32] Official Program, Casa Mañana, 1936.

[33] Stanley Green, *The World of Musical Comedy*, 4th ed. (New York: A. S. Barnes, 1980), 81, 121, 126, 152-53, 252, 255-56.

[34] Official Program, 1936.

[35] Anderson, 165. Both Rose and Anderson related similar accounts of the incident with only slight variations for ego.

[36] *Star-Telegram*, 28 May 1936, 9; Maurice obituary, 1942 (date unknown) in the vertical files of the Fort Worth Public Library, local history department. Maurice was known professionally as Hyman Maurice although his name was actually Maurice Hyman.

[37] Anderson, 161-62.

[38] Ned Alvord, letter to William Shropshire, 4 July 1958, in Tarrant Collection of the Fort Worth Public Library; Anderson, 161-62.

[39] Unattributed article, Women's Division Scrapbook, 1936, Tarrant Collection, Fort Worth Public Library. Certain articles which could be found only in the Women's Division Scrapbook are hereafter designated WDS 1936.

[40] *Press*, 23 March 1936, 8.

[41] Interview with Janice Nicolson Holmes, former Casa Mañana dancer, October 1985, Fort Worth; interview with Beth Lea Clardy, former Casa Mañana showgirl, October 1985, Fort Worth.

[42] Interview with Clardy.

[43] *Star-Telegram*, 28 April 1936, 9; Anderson, 166; Mary Martin, *My Heart Belongs*, (New York: William Morrow, 1976) 54-56; interview with Mrs. Dorothy Mefford, former Casa Mañana dancer, Fort Worth, 1993.

[44] Interview with Mefford.

[45] Interview with Phil North, son of James M. North, 3 August 1995, Fort Worth.

[46] *Star-Telegram*, 31 May 1936, 1; *Press*, 3 June 1936, 19.

[47] The sketch for the ad was done by Jewel Brannon Walker, wife of a local advertising executive.

[48] Fort Worth Frontier Centennial tri-fold advertising brochure, "Wild and Whoopee!" 1936 in the collections of the Center For American History, University of Texas, Austin.

[49] *Star-Telegram*, 16 March 1936 (eve.), 1.

[50] Conrad, 89.

[51] *Variety*, 11 March 1936, 58; John Rosenfield, *Dallas Morning News*, 8 July 1936, 10. Billy Rose also took credit for the slogan's fabrication according to Maurice Zolotow, "The Fabulous Billy Rose," *Colliers*, 1 March 1947, 52.

[52] Interview with William E. Jary, Fort Worth historian and advertising executive, October 1985. Jary worked for Corn Sign Company and did much of the planning for the sign. *Variety*, 29 May 1936, 1; 20 May 1936, 1, 54; 27 May 1936, 63; *Star-Telegram*, 10 June 1936, 22; 19 June 1936, 22; *Press*, 18 May 1936, 1.

[53] Ragsdale, 287-88; Payne, 169-70.

[54] *Austin Statesman*, 9 July 1936, 10.

[55] Telephone interviews with Jack Gordon, former amusements columnist, *Fort Worth Press*, September-October 1985, Fort Worth; *Press*, 8 June 1936, 8, 11 June 11, 11; *Austin Statesman*, 9 July 1936, 10.

[56] Unattributed story reproduced in a half-page display of articles from across the state, *Star-Telegram*, 9 August 1936, 3.

[57] *Press*, 22 May 1936, 1.

[58] *Press*, 3 June 1936, 5.

[59] Rosenfield, "The Passing Show," *Dallas Morning News* (date unknown) Sec. II, 2, Box 17, Folder 10a, Carter Collection.

[60] Rosenfield, *Dallas Morning News*, 8 July 1936, 10

• • • • • • CHAPTER FOUR • • • • • •

[1] Memo from James M. North to Amon G. Carter, 30 April 1936, Box 17, Folder 10a, Carter Collection.

[2] Telegram from James M. North to Jesse H. Jones, 15 June 1936, Box 17, Folder 10a; telegram from James M. North to Jesse H. Jones, 20 June 1936, Box 17, Folder 10a, Carter Collection.

[3] Letter from James M. North to Jesse H. Jones, 20 June 1936, Box 17, Folder 10a; letter from North to W. B. Costello, 14 June 1936, Box 17, Folder 10a, Carter Collection.

[4] Wire from Jesse H. Jones to Amon Carter, 10 July 1936, Box 17, Folder 10a, Carter Collection.

[5] Interview with Mary Wynn Wayman, former *Star-Telegram* reporter, Fort Worth, July 1996.

[6] *Time*, 8 June 1936, 12-13; *Newsweek*, 27 June 1936, 20.

[7] John Rosenfield, Jr., "The Passing Show," *Dallas Morning News*, (n.d.) Section II, p. 2, Box 17, Folder 10a, Carter Collection.

[8] Taken from various accounts including *Time*, 8 June 1936, 12-13; *Time*, 22 June 1936, 83. Colonel Houston's remarks appeared in a two-page ad in *Time* and were recorded for the "March of Time" newsreel released around 19 June 1936.

[9] *Frontier Centennial Longhorn*, special issue four-page newspaper, 4 July 1936, 1, Box 17, Folder 10a, Carter Collection.

[10] *Longhorn*, 4 July 1936, 1.

[11] "Billy Rose of New York, The Colossus of Fort Worth," *Newsweek*, 27 June 1936, 20.

[12] *New York World Telegram*, part of composite article in *Star-Telegram*, 7 May 1936, 12.

[13] John Rosenfield, *Dallas Morning News*, 8 July 1936, 1.

[14] *Press*, 18 May 1936, 3.

[15] *Press*, 2 June 1936, 9.

[16] Ibid.

[17] Thomas DeLong, *Pops: Paul Whiteman, King of Jazz* (Piscataway, N.J.: New Century, 1983), 206-08; To save money, according to Whiteman's biographer, Whiteman accepted the invitation of Amon Carter to live at Shady Oak Farm during the 1937 season.

[18] DeLong, 208; interview with former showgirl, Mrs. Mary Paige Covey Oliver, Fort Worth, August 1986

[19] Anthony Slide, *The Vaudevillians: A Dictionary of Vaudeville Performers* (Westport, Conn.: Arlington House, 1981), 57, 68.

[20] *Star-Telegram*, 26 June 1936, 5.

[21] *Star-Telegram*, 1 July 1936, 6; *Dallas Times Herald*, 1 July 1936, sec. 2, 16; Gray, 97; Rand's salary reported in *Variety*, 29 July 1936, 55.

[22] Interviews with Gordon.

[23] Phil Russell with Judy Alter, *The Quack Doctor* (Fort Worth: Branch-Smith, 1974), 24-25; interview with Stevenson.

[24] Interview with Wayman; *Austin American*, 6 July 1936, 2; *Press*, 1 July 1936, 1; 9 July 1936, 9.

[25] Interview with Wayman.

[26] Tyler [Texas] *Journal*, 3 July 1936, 5. Figures and drawings were issued by the Frontier Centennial organization in standard press releases to newspapers throughout the southwest.

[27] Unattributed article (WDS 1936).

[28] *Press*, 11 June 1936, 11.

[29] Ernie Pyle, then a roving reporter for Scripps-Howard reported the comment, *Press*, 3 June 1936, 9.

[30] Jack Gordon, *Press*, 11 June 1936, 11.

[31] Interview with Melvin O. Dacus, former general manager of Casa Mañana Musicals, Fort Worth, 1980.

[32] Unattributed article (WDS 1936).

[33] Interviews with Holmes, Clardy; interviews with Virginia Dofflemeyer Miller, Wilby Lingo Goodman, Olive Nicolson Pemberton, former Casa Manana dancers, October 1985.

[34] Zolotow, p. 312; *Star-Telegram*, 20 June 1936, 1; advertising brochure, Frontier Fiesta, 1936, Center of Texas History.

[35] Interview with Wayman.

[36] Ibid.

[37] Ibid.

[38] John H. Sorrells, *Press*, 10 July 1936, 1.

[39] *Star-Telegram*, 12 July 1936, 1, 5.

[40] *Dallas Morning News*, 18 July 1936, 1, 12.

[41] *Star-Telegram*, 2 August 1936, 11.

[42] *New York Times*, Drama section, 26 July 1936, 2.

[43] Bob Vollmer, "Flashback To Fame: The Biggest Summer Texas Ever Had," (Source and page unknown), 1946, Center For American History.

[44] John Rosenfield, Jr., *Dallas Morning News*, 18 July 1936, 1, 12; 19 July 1936, 12.

[45] Jimmy Lovell, *Dallas Times Herald*, 19 July 1936, sec. 3, 13.

[46] *Dallas Evening Journal*, 20 July 1936, 10, 11.

[47] *Press*, 18 July 1936, 7.

[48] Remark attributed to Whiteman by John Rosenfield, *Dallas Morning News*, 19 July 1936, 12.

· · · · · · CHAPTER FIVE · · · · · ·

1 *Star-Telegram*, 19 July 1936, 1; *Dallas Morning News*, 19 July 1936, 12.

2 After all the posturing by city and show officials in the neighboring cities, the *Dallas Morning News* took note of a strange phenomenon. On opening day in Fort Worth, attendance at the Dallas centennial, instead of declining, actually surged to 50,979, the highest of the entire week.

3 *Star-Telegram*, 19 July 1936, 1, 6.

4 *Star-Telegram*, 19 July 1936, 6.

5 *New York Times*, 26 July 1936, Drama sec., 2; *Star-Telegram*, 19 July 1936, 6.

6 Casa Mañana printed menu, 1936, in the collections of the author and Tarrant Collection, Fort Worth Public Library.

7 *Time*, 8 June 1936, 11-13.

8 Bob Vollmer, "Flashback To Fame: The Biggest Summer Texas Ever Had," (source and page unknown), 1946, Center For American History.

9 *Star-Telegram*, 1 June 1936 (eve.), 9; 7 July 1936, 9.

10 Vollmer.

11 *Dallas Morning News*, 19 July 1936, 12.

12 *Press*, 2 July 1936, 3; E. Clyde Whitlock, *Star-Telegram*, 19 July 1936, 7.

13 *New York Times*, 26 July 1936, Drama sec., 2.

14 Interview with Norris Mefford and Mrs. Dorothy Murray Mefford, former Casa Mañana employees, Fort Worth, August 1993.

15 Gray, 100.

16 Quoted in *Variety*, 15 July 1936, 86.

17 *Star-Telegram*, 19 July 1936, 8.

18 *New York Times*, 26 July 1936, Drama sec., 2.

19 Interviews with Gordon.

20 Nelson M. Davidson, *Pencil Trails: The Texas Centennial Exhibition in Dallas and Texas* (Dallas: Dealey and Lowe, 1936), 10; Gray, 97; *Variety*, 22 July 1936, 1; *Press*, 23 July 1936, 12; *Star Telegram*, 14 July 1936, 18.

21 *Press*, 13 June 1936, 5.

22 Unattributed article (WDS 1936); *Press*, 13 June 1936, 7.

23 *Tyler Journal*, 31 July 1936, 1; *Palestine Daily Herald*, 20 July 1936, 1.

24 *Italy News Herald*, 24 July 1936, 1.

25 *Austin Statesman*, 9 July 1936, 10; *Press*, 2 July 1936, 3.

26 Interview with North.

[27] Telegrams from Amon Carter to Henry A. Wallace, Cordell Hull, John Nance Garner, 23 July 1936, Box 17, Folder 10b, Carter Collection.

[28] Interview with Ronald Aultman, Fort Worth attorney and former Blackstone Hotel bellhop, September 1995. Aultman paid much of his way through law school with his earnings as a bell-hop during the centennial era.

[29] *Star-Telegram*, 5 August 1936, 9.

[30] *Star-Telegram*, 23 July 1936 (eve.), 4; 12 August 1936, 1; *Press*, 21 July 1936, 5; 22 July 1936, 1.

[31] Zolotow, 309-10.

[32] Rose, 21-22.

[33] *Press*, 11 August 1936, 5; 12 August 1936, 5; 20 August 1936, 12.

[34] *Press*, 29 June 1936, 1; 13 July 1936, 5; 22 July 1936, 14; 15 September 1936, 1.

[35] Telephone interview with Stevenson; *Press*, 16 July 1936, 12; *Star-Telegram*, 24 July 1936 (eve.), 4; 5 August 1936 (eve.), 3.

[36] Telephone interview with Stevenson. As a thirteen year old, she often attended the broadcasts with her father, publisher Amon Carter.

[37] *Star-Telegram*, 14 July 1936, 4; *Press*, 22 August 1936, 1.

[38] Telephone interview with Stevenson.

[39] *Star-Telegram*, 15 September 1936, 1; *Press*, 15 September 1936, 10.

[40] Telegrams from Amon Carter to Franklin Roosevelt, 22 August 1936; from John Nance Garner to Amon Carter, 25 August 1936, Box 17, Folder 10b, Carter Collection.

[41] Johnston, 31.

[42] *Variety*, 29 July 1936, 55; 26 August 1936, 95.

[43] *Variety*, 26 August 1936, 95.

[44] Jesse O. Thomas, *Negro Participation in the Texas Centennial* (Boston: Christopher Publishing, 1938), 75.

[45] Green, 122.

[46] *Press*, 31 October 1936, 1.

[47] *Press*, 3 November 1936, 12; Interviews with Holmes, Goodman.

[48] Unattributed article (WDS 1936).

* * * * * * CHAPTER SIX * * * * * *

[1] *Star-Telegram*, 9 March 1937 (eve.), 1, 6.

[2] Zolotow, 312-13.

[3] DeLong, 206-08; Robert Randol, *Star-Telegram*, 15 January 1937 (eve.), 22. Cowboy regalia and land was not all the bandleader collected. His sister-in-law, Ivy, married local doctor

William Crawford, after Crawford was hired as Whiteman's physician for the summer. Whiteman's arranger-pianist, Roy Bargy, married Virginia McLean, a local singer in the show; and his Texas singer, Durelle Alexander, married Edmund Van Zandt, Jr., son of Whiteman's landlord, Edmund Van Zandt, Sr.

[4] *Star-Telegram*, 10 October 1936, 2.

[5] The Frontier Centennial had to share the 138-acre Van Zandt plot with the Will Rogers Coliseum, Auditorium, and Memorial Tower, under construction through the end of 1936. The centennial showgrounds covered only about fifty of those acres.

[6] John E. Vacha, "Biggest Bash: Cleveland's Great Lakes Exposition," *Timeline*, March/April 1996, 18-22.

[7] Jack Gordon, *Press*, 31 May 1937, 1, 6.

[8] *Star-Telegram*, 15 January 1937, Women's Division Scrapbook, 1937. Some articles, due to mislabeling, could be found only in the Women's Division Scrapbook, 1937. Issues of the *Fort Worth Press*, June-September 1937 were lost. In both cases, these articles hereafter are labeled WDS 1937.

[9] Interviews with Goodman, Pemberton, Holmes, Clardy.

[10] Jack Gordon, *Press* 14 June 1937 (WDS 1937); *Star-Telegram*, 7 July 1937 (eve.), 19.

[11] *Star-Telegram*, 2 April 1937, 1.

[12] Quoted by Jack Gordon, *Press*, 24 June 1937 (WDS 1937).

[13] Zolotow, 328b.

[14] *Star-Telegram*, 24 September 1997, sec. B, 7, 8.

[15] *Star-Telegram*, 22 December 1975, 1; Caleb Pirtle, *Fort Worth: The Civilized West* (Tulsa: Continental Heritage, 1980), 190-91.

[16] "It Can't Happen Here" sequence in 1937 Casa Mañana based on a novel by Sinclair Lewis, *It Can't Happen Here*.

[17] Jack Gordon, *Press*, 25 March 1937 (WDS 1937).

[18] *New York Times*, 28 October 1936, 30.

[19] Lorraine Browne, "Federal Theatre: Melodrama, Social Protest, and Genius," *Quarterly Journal of the Library of Congress*, 18-37; Hallie Flanagan, *Arena: The History of the Federal Theatre* (New York: Benjamin Blom, 1940), 125-29.

[20] *Chicago Tribune*, 8 November 1936, sec. 7, 13.

[21] Vacha, 22-23; *Variety*, 30 June 1937, 60.

[22] *Star-Telegram*, 25 June 1937, 5.

[23] *Press*, 21 April 1937, 10; *Press*, 27 September 1937 (WDS 1937). Correspondence between author and Lelia S. Teixeira of Whiting and Davis, 1 September 1995. Ms. Teixeira reveals that only one time in their history did Whiting and Davis produce a "karat" gold dress. This was in 1989 for Absolut Vodka.

[24] *Star-Telegram*, 14 July 1937 (eve.), 8.

[25] *Press*, undated article (WDS 1937).

[26] The term "pickaninny," possibly from the Portugese, refers to a black child; *Press*, 23 July 1937; 31 July 1937 (WDS 1937).

[27] *Press*, 13 May 1937, 6; *Star-Telegram*, 11 June 1937 (eve.), 22.

[28] Boyce House, "Frontier Fiesta of 1937 Opens Bigger, Better," *West Texas Today*, July 1937, 1, 2, 16; *Press*, 17 July 1937 (WDS 1937); *Star-Telegram*, 17 June 1937 (eve.), 17.

[29] Unattributed article (WDS 1937).

[30] Boyce House; *Star-Telegram*, 24 June 1937, 1.

[31] *Variety*, 30 June 1937, 60.

[32] Interview with Pemberton.

[33] Quoted by Boyce House, 2.

[34] *Star-Telegram*, 30 June 1937, 1.

[35] Unattributed article (WDS 1937).

[36] John Rosenfield, *Dallas News*, 26 June 1937, sec. 1, 10.

[37] *Star-Telegram*, 11 June 1937 (eve.), 22; *Variety*, 30 June 1937, 60.

[38] *Star-Telegram*, 30 June 1937, 1; *Press*, 30 June 1937, (WDS, 1937); Interviews with Goodman, Pemberton, Holmes, Clardy.

[39] William Greg Travis, *Galen Gough: The World's Miracle Strong Man*, (Benton, KY: William Greg Travis, 1996), 87.

[40] Telephone interview with Greg Travis, June 1995; *Star-Telegram*, 30 June 1937 (eve.), 8; 2 July 1937 (eve.), 5, 9 July 1937 (eve.), 4.

[41] *The Texas Weekly*, 1 May 1937 (page unknown), WPA *Fort Worth City Guide and History*, 4J78, File 8 (page unknown), Center For American History.

[42] Unattributed article (WDS 1937).

[43] House, 2.

[44] Vacha, 15, 22.

[45] *Variety*, 30 June 1937, 60.

[46] *Press*, 31 May 1937, 1, 6; 24 June 1937 (WDS 1937), 26 June 1937 (WDS 1937); 27 June 1937 (WDS 1937); *Star-Telegram*, 26 June 1937, 1, 2; 27 June 1937, 1, 2, 4; 5 July 1937, 1; 6 July 1937, 1.

· · · · · · CHAPTER SEVEN · · · · · ·

[1] House, 1-2.

[2] John Rosenfield, *Dallas News*, 26 June 1937, sec. I, 10.

[3] "Billy Rose Puts on Two Shows In Fort Worth, Texas and in Cleveland, Ohio," *Life*, 19 July 1937, 36-39.

4 *Press*, 18 July 1937 (WDS,1937); *Star-Telegram*, 20 July 1937 (eve.), 6.

5 *Star-Telegram*, 7 July 1937 (eve.), 19.

6 Engraved invitation for Royal Box noblemen (WDS,1937). *Variety*, 30 June 1937, 61; Rose, 23-24. Michael Romanoff, a publicity chaser and impostor, claimed kinship to the deposed Russian royal family. He had immigrated to the United States from Lithuania in 1919 and subsequently built a career of sorts capitalizing on his friendships with celebrities. He eventually founded Romanoff's, an upscale Los Angeles restaurant that catered to politicians and the show business crowd.

7 *Star-Telegram*, 3 July 1937 (eve.), 11; *Variety*, 7 July 1937, 61.

8 *Star-Telegram*, 21 July 1937, 5.

9 *Star-Telegram*, 4 September 1937 (eve.), 1, 2.

10 Memo from James North to Amon Carter, 8 July 1937, Box 17, Folder 11a, Carter Collection.

11 Memo from James North to Amon Carter, 10 July 1937; second undated memo from several days later, Box 17, Folder 11a, Carter Collection.

12 Memos from James North to Amon Carter, 8 July 1937, 10 July 1937, Box 17, Folder 11a, Carter Collection.

13 Conrad, 117-18.

14 Undated memo from James North to Amon Carter, Box 17, Folder 11a, Carter Collection.

15 Interview with Norris Mefford, former Casa Mañana bartender, 1937-1938 Casa Mañana, Fort Worth, 1993.

16 *Press*, 2 July 1937 (WDS,1937), 14 July 1937 (WDS,1937), 18 July 1937 (WDS,1937), 16 August 1937 (WDS,1937); *Star-Telegram*, 24 July 1937, 8.

17 Undated letter and memo from Billy Rose to Amon Carter and James North, Box 17, Folder 11a, Carter Collection.

18 Undated memo from James North to Amon Carter, Box 17, Folder 11a, Carter Collection.

19 Memo from general manager James F. Pollock to James North, August 30, 1937, Box 17, Folder 11a, Carter Collection.

20 Bud Russell, "What Should the Laity Oppose?" *Baptist Standard*, 17 September 1936, 1, 8.

21 Bradley Allison and Troupe Reid, Annual minutes of Tarrant County Baptist Association, 1936, 11-12.

22 Ibid., 11-12.

23 Robert C. Toll, *On With the Show: The First Century of Show Business in America*, 233; *Variety*, 30 June 1937, 60.

24 *Press*, 18 July 1937 (WDS,1937), 23 July 1937 (WDS,1937); *Star-Telegram*, 25 June 1937 (eve.), 22; 6 July 1937, 8.

25 *Star-Telegram*, 26 July 1937 (eve.), 17; *Press*, 27 July (WDS,1937).

26 Transcript of phone conversation between Margaret Mitchell's attorney and Richard Brett. Macmillan Company Records, New York Public Library, Rare Manuscripts Collection,

Margaret Mitchell File, General Correspondence, Box 95, 3 August 1937; *Press*, 13 September 1937 (WDS,1937); *Star-Telegram*, 4 July 1937, sec. 2, 6; 11 September 1937, 9; Casa Mañana program, 1937.

[27] Rudy Behlmer, ed., *Memo From David O. Selznick* (New York: Viking Press, 1972), 95-96; Judy Cameron and Paul J. Christman, *The Art of Gone With the Wind* (introduction by Daniel Mayer Selznick)(New York: Prentice-Hall, 1989), 12-13.

[28] Anne Edwards, *The Road to Tara: The Life of Margaret Mitchell*, 160-62; Bob Thomas, *Selznick* (Garden City, N.Y.: Doubleday, 1970), 139.

[29] Transcript of conversation between Richard Brett and Stephens Mitchell, Macmillan Company Records, Box 95, 25 August 1937; letter to Richard Brett from Stephens Mitchell, 30 August 1937; letter to John Marsh from Richard Brett, 2 September 1937.

[30] Finis Farr, *Margaret Mitchell of Atlanta* (New York: William Morrow, 1965), 176-77; Edwards, 263-64; transcript of conversation between Richard Brett and Stephens Mitchell, Macmillan Company Records, Box 95, 25 August 1937.

[31] *Variety*, 22 September 1937, 13.

[32] *Star-Telegram*, 15 September 1937, 9; 15 September 1937 (eve.), 1; 10 May 1942, 4; *Press*, 15 September 1937 (WDS,1937).

[33] Conrad, 117; *Billy Rose's Show of Shows* Program 1937, Tarrant Collection, Fort Worth Public Library.

[34] Richard Harwell, ed., *Margaret Mitchell's Gone With the Wind Letters, 1936-1949* (New York: Macmillan, 1976), 195-96.

· · · · · · CHAPTER EIGHT · · · · · ·

[1] *Star-Telegram*, 28 January 1936, 5; 29 January 1938, 1,2; *Press*, 27 January 1938, 1; 29 January 1938, 1; 1 February 1938, 1, 6.

[2] *New York Daily Mirror*, 12 November 1937 (page unknown), Scrapbook, Casa Mañana (New York), Billy Rose Theatre Collection, File MWEZ + n.c. 25,490.

[3] Attributed to Winchell by Zolotow, 10-11.

[4] Nelson, 81.

[5] Zolotow, 331-32.

[6] Scrapbook, Billy Rose's Casa Mañana (New York), MWEZ + n.c. 25,490; *New York Daily News*, 29 January 1938 (page unknown), 8MWEZ + n.c. 26,290, folder 2, Billy Rose Theatre Collection.

[7] Nelson, 83-86.

[8] Gottlieb, 115-16; Nelson, 86-87.

[9] Nelson, 87.

[10] *Star-Telegram*, 1 June 1938, 1.

[11] *Variety*, 13 July 1938, 43; 19 July 1938, 44; 3 August 1938, 43; interview with Clardy.

[12] Taken from various accounts including *Variety*, 3 August 1938, 43; *Star-Telegram*, 7 August 1938, 6, 7; 10 August 1938, 4, 7; 11 August 1938 4, 5; 12 August 1938 5; 13 August 1938, 1, 2; 14 August 1938 5; 21 August 1938, 9; 24 August 1938, 1; 27 August 1938, 1; 28 August 1938, 1. The entertainment bill changed throughout the summer. A promotional pamphlet issued for the 1938 Casa Mañana summarizes highlights of 1936, 1937, and 1938 shows and looks forward to 1939, incorrectly listing George Burns and Gracie Allen as headliners for the 1939 show. Center For American History.

[13] Interviews with Oliver and Clardy.

[14] *Star-Telegram*, 30 July 1938, 1, 2.

[15] *Star-Telegram*, 30 July 1938, 1, 2, 4, 5.

[16] *Variety*, 3 August 1938, 43; 10 August 1938, 47.

[17] *Variety*, 17 August 1938, 53.

[18] Remark taken from an unattributed promotional pamphlet, issued in 1939 touting the 1939 Casa Mañana, Center For American History; profit and attendance figures, *Variety*, 7 September 1938, 43; *Star-Telegram*, 31 August 1938, 1, 2. *Star-Telegram* gross profit figures ran slightly higher than those announced in *Variety*—$87,671.

[19] *Star-Telegram*, 22 July 1939, 1; 5 August 1939, 1; 12 August 1939, 1; 19 August 1939, 1; 22 August 1939, 1; 22 August 1939, 1; *Variety*, 2 August 1939, 45.

[20] Interview with Dorothy Murray Mefford.

[21] *Star-Telegram*, 4 September 1939, 1-2. The newspaper carried the entire text of the president's address, pushing news concerning Casa Mañana's final performance to the bottom of page 2.

[22] *Star-Telegram*, 4 September 1939, 1; 5 September 1939, 1; *Press*, 4 September 1939, 1; 5 September 1939, 1.

[23] *Star-Telegram*, 30 October 1941 (eve.), 11; 3 November 1941 (eve.), 10; 4 November 1941 (eve.), 3; 5 November 1941 (eve.), 1.

[24] *Press*, 11 May 1942, 6; 15 May 1942, 16; *Star-Telegram*, 10 May 1942, 4.

[25] *Star-Telegram*, 10 May 1942, 4.

[26] *Press*, 11 May 1942, 6; 15 May 1942, 16.

· · · · · · CHAPTER NINE · · · · · ·

[1] Ordinance 2378, City of Fort Worth, 5 September 1945, Fort Worth City Hall.

[2] Howard Taubman, *The Making of the American Theatre* (New York: Coward-McCann, 1967), 266.

[3] David Dachs, "Ten Years of the Music Tents," *Saturday Review*, 31 May 1958, 38.

[4] Dachs, 37.

[5] Dachs, 39.

[6] *Star-Telegram*, 12 March 1958, 3; Fort Worth Opera Association, "Casa Mañana '58," unpublished four-page brochure presented to Fort Worth City Council, November 1957, Fort Worth

Public Library. The name Casa Mañana Productions was changed before the 1958 season to Casa Mañana Musicals.

[7] The actual site of the original amphitheater lay approximately 100 feet to the south of the domed theater constructed in 1958.

[8] *Star-Telegram* and *Press*, 6 July 1958, 1; "Stage Struck Texas," *Life*, 22 December 1958, 122.

BIBLIOGRAPHY

• • • • • • BOOKS • • • • • •

Anderson, John Murray. *Out Without My Rubbers: The Memoirs of John Murray Anderson* (as told to and written by Hugh Abercrombie Anderson). New York: Library Publishers, 1954.

Behlmer, Rudy, ed. *Memo From David O. Selznick*. New York: Viking Press, 1972.

Bordman, Gerald. *The Oxford Companion to American Theatre*, 2nd Edition. New York: Oxford University Press, 1992.

Cameron, Judy and Paul J. Christman. *The Art of Gone With the Wind*, (introduction by Daniel Mayer Selznick). New York: Prentice-Hall, 1989.

Conrad, Earl. *Billy Rose: Manhattan Primitive*. Cleveland: World Publishing, 1968.

Davidson, Nelson M. *Pencil Trails: The Texas Centennial Exhibition In Dallas and Texas*. Dallas: Dealey and Lowe, 1936.

DeLong, Thomas. *Pops: Paul Whiteman, King of Jazz*. Piscataway, N.J.: New Century, 1983.

Edwards, Anne. *Road To Tara: The Life of Margaret Mitchell*. New York: Dell, 1983.

Farr, Finis. *Margaret Mitchell of Atlanta*. New York: William Morrow, 1965.

Flanagan, Hallie. *Arena: The History of the Federal Theatre*. New York: Benjamin Blom, 1940.

Flemmons, Jerry. *Amon: The Life of Amon Carter, Sr. of Texas*. Austin: Jenkins, 1978.

Fort Worth In Story and Picture. Fort Worth: Pioneer, 1936.

Garrett, Julia Kathryn. *Fort Worth: A Frontier Triumph*. Austin: Encino Press, 1972; Fort Worth: TCU Press, 1996.

Gottlieb, Polly Rose. *The Nine Lives of Billy Rose*. New York: Crown, 1968.

Green, Stanley. *The World of Musical Comedy*, Fourth edition. New York: A. S. Barnes, 1980.

Harwell, Richard, ed. *Margaret Mitchell's Gone With the Wind Letters, 1936-1949*. New York: Macmillan, 1976.

Hill, Patricia Evridge. *Dallas: The Making of a Modern City*. Austin: University of Texas Press, 1996.

Jasen, David A. *Tin Pan Alley*. New York: Donald I. Fine, 1988.

Kernfeld, ed. *The New Grove Dictionary of Jazz*. New York: St. Martin's Press, 1994.

Knight, Oliver. *Fort Worth: Outpost On the Trinity*. Norman: University of Oklahoma Press, 1953; Fort Worth: Texas Christian University Press, 1990.

Maney, Richard. *Fanfare: The Confessions of a Press Agent*. New York: Harper, 1957.

Martin, Mary. *My Heart Belongs*. New York: Morrow, 1976.

Nelson, Stephen. *Only a Paper Moon: The Theatre of Billy Rose*. Ann Arbor, Michigan: UMI Research Press, 1987.

Paddock, Captain B. B., ed. *History of Texas*, Volume III, *Fort Worth and the Texas Northwest*. Chicago: Lewis, 1922.

Pirtle, Caleb. *Fort Worth: The Civilized West*. Tulsa: Continental Heritage Press, 1980.

Payne, Darwin. *Big D: Triumphs and Troubles of an American Supercity in the 20th Century*. Dallas: Three Forks Press, 1994.

Ragsdale, Kenneth B. *The Year America Discovered Texas: Centennial '36*. College Station: Texas A&M University Press, 1987.

Rose, Billy. *Wine, Women and Words*. New York: Simon and Schuster, 1948.

Russell, Phil, with Judy Alter. *The Quack Doctor*. Fort Worth: Branch-Smith, 1974.

Serling, Robert J. *Eagle: The Story of American Airlines*. New York: St. Martin's Press, 1985.

Slide, Anthony. *The Vaudevillians: A Dictionary of Vaudeville Performers*. Westport, Conn.: Arlington House, 1981.

Talbert, Robert H. *Cowtown Metropolis: Fort Worth: Case Study of a City's Growth and Structure*. Leo Potishman Foundation: Texas Christian University, 1956.

Taubman, Howard. *The Making of the American Theatre*. New York: Coward-McCann, 1967.

Thomas, Bob. *Selznick*. Garden City, N. J.: Doubleday, 1970.

Thomas, Jesse O. *Negro Participation in the Texas Centennial*. Boston: Christopher Publishing, 1938.

Toll, Robert C. *On With the Show: The First Century of Show Business*. New York: Oxford University Press, 1976.

Travis, Greg. *Galen Gough: The World's Miracle Strong Man*. Benton, Kentucky: Greg Travis, 1996.

Van Zandt, K. M. *Force Without Fanfare: The Autobiography of K. M. Van Zandt*. Edited and annotated by Sandra L. Myres. Fort Worth: Texas Christian University, 1968.

Vidal-Naquet, Pierre, ed. *Harper Atlas of World History*. New York: Harper and Row, 1987.

WPA Fort Worth City Guide and History. N.d.

· · · · · · NEWSPAPERS · · · · · ·

Austin Statesman. Various issues, 1936.

Austin Weekly Democratic Statesman. 16 November 1876.

Billboard. Various issues, 1936-1937.

Chicago Tribune. 8 November 1936.

Dallas Evening Journal. 20 July 1936.

Dallas Morning News. Various issues, 1936-1937.

Dallas Times Herald. Various issues, 1936-1937.

Fort Worth Democrat. 6 November, 1875.

Fort Worth Press. Various issues, 1936-1939; 1958.

Fort Worth Star-Telegram. Various issues, 1936-1942, 1945-1946, 1954-1958, 1986, 1997.

Frontier Centennial Longhorn. Special issue four-page newspaper, 4 July 1936, Box 17, Folder 10a, Amon Carter Collection, Amon Carter Museum, Fort Worth, Texas.

Italy [Texas] *News Herald.* 24 July 1936.

New York Daily Mirror. 12 November 1937.

New York Daily News. 29 January 1938; 8 September 1947.

New York Times. 26 July 1936.

Palestine [Texas] *Daily Herald.* 20 July 1936.

Texas Weekly. 1 May 1937.

Tyler [Texas] *Journal.* 3 July 1936; 31 July 1936.

Variety. Various issues, 1936-1939.

· · · · · · PERIODICALS · · · · · ·

Allison, Gordon. "Music Circus." *Theatre Arts,* June 1951, 87-89.

"Billy Rose Puts On Two Shows In Fort Worth, Texas, and Cleveland, Ohio." *Life,* 19 July 1937, 36-39.

Browne, Lorraine. "Federal Theatre: Melodrama, Social Protest, and Genius." *Quarterly Journal of the Library of Congress.* 36 No.1 Winter 1979, 18-37.

Dachs, David. "Ten Years of the Music Tents." *Saturday Review,* 31 May 1958, 37-38.

"Fair Without Pants." *Time.* 31 July 1933, 20.

"Grand National." *Time.* 27 March 1933, 20-21.

Letters to the Editor. "Publisher Carter of Texas." *Time.* 20 November 1933.

Johnston, Alva. "Colonel Carter of Cartersville." *Saturday Evening Post,* 26 November 1938, 8.

Russell, Bud. "What Should the Laity Oppose?" *Baptist Standard,* 17 September 1936, 1, 8.

"Stage Struck Texas," *Life.* 22 December 1958, 122.

Time, 8 June 1936, 10-13.

Time, 22 June 1936, 82-83.

Vacha, John E. "Biggest Bash: Cleveland's Great Lakes Exposition." *Timeline.* March/April 1996, 18-22.

Vollmer, Bob. "Flashback To Fame: The Biggest Summer Texas Ever Had," source unknown, 1946, Barker History Center, University of Texas, Austin.

Zolotow, Maurice. "The Fabulous Billy Rose." *Colliers*, 1 March 1947, 44+.

· · · · · · PUBLIC RECORDS AND UNPUBLISHED WORKS · · · · · ·

Allison, Bradley and Troupe Reid. Minutes. Tarrant County Baptist Association, Southwestern Baptist Theological Seminary Library, Fort Worth.

Casa Mañana, Engraved invitation to dance with "Royal Box" nobility, 1937, Tarrant Collection, Fort Worth Public Library, Fort Worth.

Fort Worth Opera Association. "Casa Mañana 1958." Unpublished four-page brochure presented to Fort Worth City Council, November, 1957, Tarrant Collection, Fort Worth Public Library, Fort Worth.

Gray, Lois. *History of the Fort Worth Centennial*. Unpublished master's thesis, Texas Christian University, 1938.

McGilvray, Byron Wendol. *A Brief History of the Development of Music In Fort Worth, 1849-1972*. Unpublished master's thesis, Lamar University, 1972.

Menu, Casa Mañana, 1936, Tarrant Collection, Fort Worth Public Library, Fort Worth.

Minutes. Fort Worth City Council. 1935-1936.

Minutes. Executive committee, Texas Centennial Committee, 1934. Box 39, Folder 13, Amon Carter Collection, Amon Carter Museum, Fort Worth.

Minutes. Texas Centennial Committee, 1934-1935. Box 39, Folder 13, Amon Carter Collection, Amon Carter Museum, Fort Worth, Texas.

Official Program, *Billy Rose's Show of Shows*, 1937, Tarrant Collection.

Official Program, Casa Mañana, 1936, Tarrant Collection.

Official Program, Casa Mañana, 1937, Tarrant Collection.

Official Program, *Jumbo*, 1936, Tarrant Collection.

Ordinance 2378, City of Fort Worth, September 5, 1945, Fort Worth City Hall.

Program, Testimonial Luncheon Honoring Paul Whiteman and his Orchestra, given by The Fort Worth Chamber of Commerce, October 9, 1936, in the private collection of Mr. Dalton Hoffman, Fort Worth, Texas.

Zolotow, Maurice. *Billy Rose of Broadway*. Unpublished manuscript, Billy Rose Theatre Collection, New York Public Library.

· · · · · · MISCELLANEOUS SOURCES · · · · · ·

Casa Mañana Board of Control, "Casa Mañana Marches On: Texas's Greatest Open Air Theatre," Advertising pamphlet, (1939), Center For American History, University of Texas, Austin, Texas.

Board of Control, Fort Worth Frontier Fiesta Brochure, January, 1936.

Women's Division, Texas Frontier Centennial and Casa Mañana, Billy Rose Scrapbook, 1936, Tarrant Collection, Fort Worth Public Library, Fort Worth, Texas.

Women's Division, Texas Frontier Centennial and Casa Mañana, Billy Rose Scrapbook, 1937, Tarrant Collection, Fort Worth Public Library, Fort Worth, Texas.

· · · · · · · CORRESPONDENCE · · · · · · ·

Alvord, Ned. Letter to William Shropshire, 4 July 1958. Tarrant Collection, Fort Worth Public Library, Fort Worth.

Brett, Richard. Transcript of phone conversation with Margaret Mitchell's attorney, 3 August 1937. MacMillan Company Records, New York Public Library, Rare Manuscripts Collection, Margaret Mitchell File, General Correspondence, Box 95.

_____.Transcript of conversation with Stephens Mitchell, 25 August 1937. Macmillan Company Records.

_____. Letter to John Marsh, 2 September 1937. MacMillan Company Records.

Carter, Amon. Telegrams to Henry A. Wallace, Cordell Hull, John Nance Garner, 23 July 1936. Box 17, Folder 10b, Amon Carter Collection. Amon Carter Museum, Fort Worth.

_____. Letter to Walter Holbrook. Box 17, Folder 10, Amon Carter Collection. Amon Carter Museum, Fort Worth.

_____. Letter to Fritz Lanham, 12 July 1935. Box 39, Folder 13, Amon Carter Collection, Amon Carter Museum, Fort Worth.

_____. Telegram to Franklin Roosevelt, 22 August 1936. Box 17, Folder 10b, Amon Carter Collection, Fort Worth.

_____. Memo to James Record, 8 April 1936. Box 17, Folder 10, Amon Carter Collection, Fort Worth.

_____. Telegram to Jock Whitney, 4 March 1936. Box 17, Folder 10, Amon Carter Collection, Fort Worth.

Garner, John Nance. Telegram to Amon Carter, 25 August 1936. Amon Carter Collection.

Fuller, James C. Letter to members of board of directors, Casa Mañana Musicals, Inc., Fort Worth, 15 September 1964. In files of Casa Mañana Musicals.

Jones, Jesse H. Telegram to Amon Carter, 10 July 1936. Box 17, Folder 10a, Amon Carter Collection, Fort Worth.

Kramer, Arthur L. Letter to William Monnig, 19 March 1936. Box 17, Folder 10b, Amon Carter Collection, Fort Worth.

Martin, Lowry. Letter to all members of the Advisory Board, 26 July 1934. Box 39, Folder 13, Amon Carter Collection, Amon Carter Museum, Fort Worth.

Mitchell, Stephens. Letter to Richard Brett, 30 August 1937. MacMillan Company Records.

Monnig, William. Letter to Arthur L. Kramer, (N.d.) Box 17, Folder 10b, Amon Carter Collection, Fort Worth.

North, James M. Memo to Amon Carter, 30 April 1936. Amon Carter Collection, Fort Worth.

_____. Memos to Amon Carter, 8 July 1937; 10 July 1937; additional undated memos. Box 17, Folder 11a, Amon Carter Collection. Amon Carter Museum, Fort Worth.

_____. Telegram to Jesse H. Jones, 15 June 1936. Box 17, Folder 10a, Amon Carter Collection. Amon Carter Museum, Fort Worth.

_____. Telegram to Jesse H. Jones, 20 June 1936, Box 17, Folder 10a, Amon Carter Collection. Amon Carter Museum, Fort Worth.

_____. Letter to W. B. Costello, 14 July 1936. Box 17, Folder 10a, Amon Carter Collection, Fort Worth.

_____. Interoffice memos to Amon Carter, Box 17, Folder 11a, Amon Carter Collection, Fort Worth.

_____. Letter to S. H. McCarty, 1 June 1934. Box 39, Folder 13, Amon Carter Collection, Amon Carter Museum, Fort Worth.

Pollock, James F. Memo to James North, 30 August 1937. Box 17, Folder 11a, Amon Carter Collection. Amon Carter Museum, Fort Worth.

Rose, Billy. Memo to Amon Carter, 4 April 1936. Box 17, Folder 10, Amon Carter Collection, Fort Worth.

_____. Letter and memo to Amon Carter and James North (N.d.). Box 17, Folder 11a, Amon Carter Collection. Amon Carter Museum, Fort Worth.

Teixeira, Lelia S. (representative of Whiting and Davis, New York jewelers). Letter to author, 1 September 1995.

Thomas, Cullen F. Letter to Amon G. Carter, 5 January 1934. Box 39, Folder 13, Amon Carter Collection, Amon Carter Museum, Fort Worth.

· · · · · · INTERVIEWS · · · · · ·

Ronald Aultman. Interview by author. Fort Worth, August 1996.

Beth Lea Clardy. Interview by author. Tape recording. Fort Worth, October 1985.

Melvin O. Dacus. Interview by author. Fort Worth, 1980.

C. E. "Bud" Franks. Interview by author. Fort Worth, 1980.

James C. Fuller. Interview by author. Fort Worth, 1980.

Mrs. Wilby Lingo Goodman. Tape recorded interview by author. Fort Worth, October 1985.

Jack Gordon. Tape recorded interview by author. Fort Worth, September-October 1985.

Janice Nicolson Holmes. Tape recorded interview by author. Fort Worth, October 1985.

William E. Jary. Interview by author. Fort Worth, October 1985.

Dorothy Murray Mefford. Interview by author. Fort Worth, August 1993.

Norris Mefford. Interview by author. Fort Worth, August 1993.

Virginia Dofflemeyer Miller. Tape recorded interview by author. Fort Worth, August 1986.

Phil North. Tape recorded interview by author. Fort Worth. 3 August 1995.

Mary Paige Covey Oliver. Interview by author. Tape recording. Fort Worth, October 1985.

Olive Nicolson Pemberton. Tape recorded interview by author. Fort Worth, October 1985.

Michael Pollock. Interview by author. Austin, 1980.

Ruby Schmidt. Interview by author. Fort Worth, 1980

Ruth Carter Stevenson. Telephone interview by author. November 1997.

Greg Travis. Telephone interview by author. June 1995.

Loyd L. Turner. Interview by author. Fort Worth, 1980.

Mary Wynn Wayman. Tape recorded interview by author. July 1996.

ABOUT THE AUTHOR

Jan Jones is a Fort Worth native who has taught theater and English in the Metroplex for almost thirty years. Her interest in Casa Mañana began in 1980 when she wrote her master's thesis on the current theater-in-the-round. This is her first book.